MW00633237

"The *110 Philosophy* is relatable to anything ⟨...⟩ work, etc. It's all so intertwined and impacts the rest. What a great life motto to share with people of all ages and backgrounds. I can certainly see the book being relevant to entrepreneurs, business people, college students, high school students...."

~ Brendan O'Hazo, Franchise Owner of two Aroma Joe's Coffee

"The *110 Philosophy* makes yourself a top priority. Luanne gives us tools such as how to problem solve and process the impact and to do contingency planning to alleviate our anxieties and worries. This is a model to help live a happier life. I would recommend this book to anyone who is open to learning some new ways to ultimately deal with tasks at hand which are presented to us every state of life."

~ Elizabeth McGrady, Professional Organizer and Life Coach

"This is a very easy to read self-help book that I feel can be used in all areas of life. Your story in itself gives hope to always look at the 'glass half full – not half empty.' This little book is full of easy to remember guiding principles. I know it will help me in my daily home and work life."

**~ Pam Varney, Customer Service Representative,
Moody's Collision Centers**

"Just reading this book really taught me a lot. I can't wait to do all the exercises – that was a great idea! You are a very inspiring woman. Everyone who reads this book is going to learn something – I know I did! I now have the mindset that I'm going to live to be 110 years young! Thank you."

**~ Avery Paul, CEO of House Hold of 3 and one in the making,
Student and Customer Service Representative**

"The *110 Philosophy* is an awesome book! If you are starting a new adventure or need to be energized to keep going to your finish line, this is a great instruction book. Luanne lays out a great structure of how to reduce stress and keep focus on the goal at hand while balancing all the daily challenges. She is an inspiration! She has overcome several challenges that may have stopped most of us from going forward but she used her challenges to grow and stayed focus on her goal! Thank you so much for the courage to share with us."

~ Brenda Flagg Insurance Agency, Inc, East Syracuse, NY

"The best part of this book is her inspiring quotes, effective exercises and real life examples on how she got to her better life/vision. She breaks this problem/challenge into steps: what is the situation at hand, why is it happening, what needs to change and what are the possible solutions to fix it. It made sense and it worked!"

~ Jennifer Daruszka, Single Working Mom

"Life can be a challenge – take the time to read the 110 Philosophy. The tools that Luanne suggests will help bring balance and fun back into your life!"

~ Flora Bayley, Office Manager

The 110 Philosophy™

Be your best you!

Luanne Cameron

*Make to day
count !!*

*Luanne
Cameron*

TOWER
PUBLISHING

For permission to use any material from this book or product, submit a request to: Luanne Cameron, Naples, ME
www.110Philosophy.com

ISBN-13: 978-1-7339302-6-0

Contributor & Editor:
Noelle Castle, Castle Media Co.

Cover Designed by:
Rebecca Blaesing Design LLC

10 9 8 7 6 5 4 3 2

Printed in the United States of America.

Table of Contents

PERSONAL STORY

When I was a young girl, I grew up in the suburbs of Rutland, Vermont as part of a family that was the envy of the neighborhood. My dad was a successful account manager for one of the largest technology firms in the world, IBM. My mom was an intelligent and gorgeous woman who took the utmost care of my brother and me. My memories of this time include wonderful Christmases huddled around the tree opening gifts as a family. There were also numerous trips to Pennsylvania to visit my grandparents. They founded and managed a 400-bed nursing home. I gained an immense appreciation for the elderly and the longevity they embodied from these visits. My grandmother was a saint and was by far the most positive force in my young life.

Sometimes, good things, like this idyllic situation, come to an end. Our 'perfect family' situation came tumbling down when my mom had an affair with my dad's best friend when I was ten years old. My family was torn apart. My brother, being fourteen years old, was at an age that he could decide with whom he wanted to live. He chose to go live with my dad. Since I was ten years old, state law determined that I was to live with my mom and her new husband, my dad's best friend.

Mom's new husband was a terror and pedophile. On a number of occasions, he forced me into sexually abusive situations. For fun, and to watch me sweat, he once forced me to spend an afternoon moving a pile of bricks five feet across the yard. My family's financial stability was also shattered. We quickly wound up far from the suburbs in the Vermont backwoods, living in a shack, bathing in the river and using an outhouse. While we eventually moved into a trailer home, as winter approached, my sense of loss and ruin was complete. It took me many years to recover from these childhood traumas.

From this rocky collapse of my childhood, I was inspired to take a goal-oriented approach to life that helped me to ensure my own family didn't go down the same path that my parents' family had followed. When I started dating, I dated with the intention of finding a partner to marry. I knew I wanted to find someone who would provide stability, true-life long companionship and support for our children in a way my parents weren't able to. I became extremely focused on my career and worked hard to ensure that I would never again be destitute. Fortunately, I found my soul mate and best friend. We started a loving family, raising two boys of our own. My career took off as I completed several major start-up operations for large insurance companies and became an executive in the industry. I was also determined to live a long life, inspired by the kindly longevity of my grandmother and her nursing home neighbors.

The vision for life and iron clad discipline I gained from my childhood has helped me overcome numerous obstacles later on in my life. This included the disintegration of my career as I exited corporate life at the height of the Great Recession and spent eighteen months unemployed; a battle with breast cancer and a lifesaving mastectomy; and several other health challenges that required eight surgeries and numerous bed-ridden months of recovery. These challenges have forced me to refine my goals and constantly remind myself of my vision for life. They have required me to put into fine clarity the reasons why I stay engaged in the daily grind of life and have instilled in me a sense of disciplined structure that helps me get through the day.

With this book, I am taking the next step in my own personal pursuit of growth by sharing with you my formula for successful living. I am determined to help others find meaning in their own lives. The principles, tips, and techniques contained in these pages are the product of a life that has seen hardship and success. I have named the techniques found in this book the *110 Phil0sophy* because I believe they can help anyone get 110% out of their days and can help everyone start living like they'll make it to 110 years young.

Thank you for taking the time to pick up this book and consider the learnings I've put down here. If you stick with the Guiding Principles given in these pages, you will begin to lead a life that is motivated by your passion and is committed to achieving your own goals.

Welcome to The *110 Philosophy*!

The *110 Philosophy*™ is a proven management methodology for business and personal success – an approach to life that will help you manage through all the challenges, and experience better relationships, more success, and be a better leader.

"A proven method to create more happiness in your life – NOW!"
~ Luanne Cameron

It starts with having a clear vision, and then engaging 110% in living that vision. **My Vision** is to live to be 110 years young! This clear vision is the reason I named my business and my philosophy the *110 Philosophy* – to keep my vision front and foremost – and to remind me what I am striving for every day in everything I do!

The *110 Philosophy* provides a road map to create discipline and structure in life and work in order to get 110% out of every moment:

- Focus on goals
- Manage time wisely
- Make good decisions
- Reduce stress
- Improve relationships
- Harness greater energy
- Achieve success and satisfaction in life and work!

Have you noticed that the book is starting on page 110? Good for you – you're already using your senses to differentiate how life throws you curves and how to handle them!

One of the reasons for this different pagination is to teach the value of keeping the end in sight as you live your life or while you build an organization or cooperation.

Another teaching lesson of the book is the value of being present. By turning each page, one by one, counting down to page 1, you will start the engagement of this learning process!

Also, I love Robert Frost's poem, "The Road Not Taken."

"Two roads diverged in a wood, and I – I took the one less traveled by, and that has made all the difference."

~ Robert Frost

I would only add to his poem…build in FUN along the way (or in everything you do)…so here's to adding a little fun in flipping the pages of a new way of thinking!

How would you like to change your life NOW?!

Introduction

The primary audience for this book is geared towards professionals, business leaders and small business owners who might be looking for direction or feel overwhelmed by distractions. There are so many interferences in today's everyday life and people are caught up in indecisiveness and distractions every second, every minute, every hour of the day. People don't know where they're going in life and are challenged with figuring out their purpose.

I personally grew professionally from a large corporation environment career to being a successful small business owner for the last 10 years. I feel for so many small business owners who are working so hard day in and day out. And yet, they struggle with indecisiveness when faced with numerous challenges because they lack the direction and vision to move them forward.

Basically, I wrote this book just to help people. I have been challenged over and over, and over again in my life. I believe my true purpose in life is simple, to help others be their best they can be!

And perhaps the main reason I wrote this book was as simple as helping me get through the last 10 years of some unbelievable chain of chronic illnesses after overcoming a crazy childhood experience. And then I stepped out of my incredibly successful executive career, in the thick of the recession, losing 80% of my household income. Perhaps I just had to figure out my true purpose for all this craziness in my life! And if I can figure out how to navigate through the minutia, the distractions and the crazy challenges of life and be happy, perhaps this was the purpose of all my life challenges…if I can do it, so can you!

So why was it so important to me to deliver this manuscript on 1/10/2020? Because it summarizes in numbers all that this book represents. On January 10, 2020, this book will be published worldwide! This book is all about using your past experiences to make your future much more clear and bright. I couldn't think of a better day to deliver my message – the message of both doing 110% and "hind sight is 20/20!"

Taking on this effort to share my message through writing a book has been an incredible challenge over the last five years. I needed to deliver my message and complete this goal! I know the power of goals (1.10.2020), and I know the power of a vision. I do hope I help at least 110 individuals with my message!

The Story behind the Turtle!

Turtles have always had a special place in my heart, starting from when I was very little. My childhood nickname was "Turtle" – as I was a VERY slow eater!

But beyond that, I have several wonderful childhood memories of finding them; and then, I seemed to find them more and more over the years of my life. Their connections to nature are very similar to my life experiences. I love their longevity, their ability to endure the unimaginable and still continue on their path to nurture their own life so they can nurture those around them for generations to come!

By the time you finish this book, you will have learned about the power behind visuals. For me, turtles have been a very personal and powerful visual – representing perseverance, endurance, and so much more! In addition to the turtle symbolization, you might see the hidden visual on the book's front cover. As you read on, you'll discover that visual's meaning within this book.

As you know, there are all types of turtles, most of them are slow – which is an incredible trait, as slow and steady tends to win the race. However, I have so enjoyed the sea turtles. Their grace and speed is admirable. We can all learn from turtles of all types across the world as long as we remain open to see the value they offer and the beauty behind their tough little shell!

110 Philosophy

The Secret to Happiness in Any Situation

The *110 Philosophy* is a **simple** approach to help individuals manage their way successfully through life's challenges, both personally and professionally. Employing the *110 Philosophy* in your life will give you the tools to change your challenges into valuable opportunities to make your life better—a life of happiness. The amazing news?! Within ourselves, we each have everything necessary to do so already! All you need are the right methods. This book will provide you with the essential techniques you need. With these techniques you will: learn to **prioritize your time** differently in order to reach your goals; **manage your thinking** so your reaction to situations is positive and productive; and, **make decisions effectively** and quickly so you can move on and not get bogged down. The *110 Philosophy* will open up your mind to experience more happiness NOW!

How can the *110 Philosophy* help me?

The *110 Philosophy* is an attitude and perspective on life that will help you focus on your goals and manage your time wisely. Fundamentally, it's about enriching your life and getting 110% out of every moment. When you employ the principles of the *110 Philosophy* in your daily behavior, you WILL experience more success in your work and personal life!

Stop letting the downs and outs of everyday life circumstances spoil your happiness or determine your quality of life. The *110 Philosophy* will teach you how to turn around these challenges and get you out of negative thinking. You will learn to approach your thinking in a new and powerful way, developing a mindset for success and happiness in your life that is in *your* control. In your career, personal life, and in the relationships that surround you – you have the choice to let events derail you or to see obstacles as opportunities. Employ the *110 Philosophy* to start living a happier, healthier, and more successful life – NOW.

The *110 Philosophy* provides a road map to create discipline and structure in life, as well as work, in order to get 110% out of every moment based on the implementation and execution of these five Guiding Principles:

---

110 Philosophy Guiding Principles:

1. **Spirituality**
2. **Self**
3. **Spouse/Key Partnership**
4. **Family/Friendships**
5. **Career**

These guidelines will then help you to:

- Focus on goals
- Manage time wisely
- Make good decisions
- Reduce stress
- Improve relationships
- Harness greater energy
- Achieve success and satisfaction in life and work!

The *110 Philosophy* will help you become disciplined and will bring structure to your hectic schedule. It will focus your energy towards things that matter most in life, but all too often get put off for another day. You will experience better relationships, more success, and be a better leader. You can stop putting off the things that really matter for another day. You can stop wondering when you will find happiness.

Be the good that the world needs right now.

Every day, be somebody's reason to believe the world is a good place – a place to smile and to laugh. I always work to show a little extra appreciation and kindness to others I encounter. This is not "being fake." I sincerely appreciate that everybody has struggles, and I have no idea what that person checking me out at the cash register has going on in their life. Especially someone grumpy and grouchy – I make it my mission to make them laugh or at least get a smile out of them!

I remember very clearly when I learned the value of making people smile. I was in line at the grocery store and I turned and there was a Veteran wearing a Vietnam cap. I reached out to shake his hand and said, "Thank you very much for your service!" The gentleman began to get very emotional and told me I had no idea how good I was making him feel. This experience had a tremendous impact on me! I realized that it was not only about how I was making someone else feel, but how I was making *myself* feel. So that year, making others smile became one of my New Year's Resolutions – because that act would add the structure to the goal, and hold me more accountable to do it (more on Structure later!) I'm always thinking forward to how I can become a better person, and this goal impacts my life as much as I impact other people. When we work to make someone else happy, it makes us happy!

Remember, *you always have a choice* to either see the good in the world, or the bad. See the positive in any given situation or the negative. Why not see the good?! Why not see the opportunity to improve or learn?! No matter where I am, I try to remember to smile, look people in the eye, talk to people, say thank you, and if possible to compliment them on something. Making people feel like they matter is a great gift, and it's free!

Everyone has their own challenges,

be kind!

Make a difference, be the change.

110 Philosophy

Are YOU ready to get started?!

The *110 Philosophy* is an approach to life that will help you manage through all of life's challenges, large and small. I know because I have tested it! These are strategies that I have used in my own life, during the most difficult times – childhood abuse, my parents' divorce, a dramatic departure from my corporate career, two life-threatening illness diagnoses (breast cancer and a rare autoimmune disease) that both required invasive surgeries and long, painful recoveries. Like so many people, the list goes on! My point here is not to wallow or pull a "woe is me" card – my point is that *everybody's* life is full of highs and lows! It truly is how you deal with those highs and lows that will determine their effect on your happiness. No one can avoid or escape the down times. We can over-indulge in the good times and take them for granted, and we can wallow in self-pity during the hard times and learn nothing from them. That doesn't work for me.

I realized that I had developed a unique way to handle the ups and downs in my own life. I am an action-oriented person, so when I have a dilemma I set about figuring out how to fix it. One of my mottos is, "Keep it moving" – I don't like to stay stuck in inde-cisiveness or negativity. When I recognize I am getting bogged down in a matter, I go into problem-solving mode. As I talked to people about my approach to life, coached my team through conflicts and challenges, spoke to colleagues about how I ran my business, the reactions had consistently some degree of surprise and awe. *"How do you do it?!"* I was asked over and over again. What had become second nature approaches to dealing with challenges and fully appreciating good times for me were tools other people needed to get through their own lives. I started really paying attention to how I processed experiences in my life, how I moved myself from struggling to resolving. When I shared what I did, how I thought through experiences, *it worked* for others and they came back for more! I realized I was onto something! What I now call the *110 Philosophy*, is essentially my approach to life, packaged in simple, quick (because I don't like to waste time *at all*!) methods I use in my daily life – to turn things around quickly so I do not get stuck in the negatives, but get the best out of my life, enjoy my relationships and my work, and experience happiness – *real* happiness!

All of the techniques of the *110 Philosophy* are *easy* – life is already too complicated! For any real change to occur in life, it needs to be something you can pull out of your proverbial toolbox fast, otherwise we just get trapped in over-thinking behavior loops that get us nowhere. You do not need to take a week off from work to figure this out, or sequester yourself away from your family all weekend to complete assignments, before you can get started implementing the *110 Philosophy* in your life. In fact, I'm giving you your first cool, new tool at the end of this section – a quick exercise that will allow you to boost your satisfaction and happiness in your life *right now*!

The *110 Philosophy* in a Nutshell

What I know for sure to be true is that when my life feels out of balance, when my happiness meter is running way too low, that is when I get stuck in over-thinking and let my thoughts get irrational (catastrophizing, we all do it!) That is when I get too distracted by feelings, thoughts and activities outside of the issue at hand. *What changes all that* – when I get back to what my vision is for my life, I consistently apply a structure to keep my priorities in check, and I discipline myself to follow my plan and – *get myself back on course*, if you will. The *110 Philosophy* is all about controlling our thoughts, which control our behaviors! The only thing standing between you and your happiness is your attitude when you encounter challenges. The difference between getting down and staying there and managing your thinking so you move to a more positive reaction to life's trials, is your thinking. Learn to manage your thoughts and you control your happiness. In your work, as a professional, you can manage your workload, your to-do list, and your work-life balance better. As a leader, you will lead by example, and manage your staff better because they will have a clear role model to follow. That may sound too good to be true, but I assure you it's not because I live it every day. Read on and I'll teach you exactly what you need to do to change your thinking patterns, and in turn, change your life!

The *110 Philosophy* works in all areas of life because it operates on our fundamental needs as humans which I call our **Guiding Principles**. It requires that you have laser-focused vision and determination for a clear **Vision** to keep your life on track, personally and professionally, and then apply a disciplined way of thinking through challenges to solve problems. The *110 Philosophy* translates so well to business because leaders must offer a vision and build engagement with their team about where a business is going. Goodness knows businesses encounter plenty of problems, and the specific problem-solving strategies of the *110 Philosophy* will work through those quickly and efficiently. We all need a system in place to keep us focused and help measure our results. This is the only way to positively move forward in our lives and work.

The *110 Philosophy* provides balance in life and work!

- When you have a clear **Vision**, and the **Structure** and **Discipline** in place to stay focused on your vision, you WILL have more balance in your life as well as more productivity in the workplace. This in turn develops into a great office culture.

- The **Guiding Principles** are the foundation of the *110 Philosophy* and provide a **Structure** for the necessary attention to key areas of life in our daily decision-making.

- Utilizing the **Guiding Principles** consistently provides the ability to remain laser-focused and minimize distractions.

- Balance is achieved by having a check-and-balance mechanism built into life to alert you when your priorities are off.

- Utilizing daily **Discipline** in how you react to events, make decisions, and set your priorities is your path to success and achieving the happiness you desire.

Summing it all up in a visual for you – the *110 Philosophy* looks like this:

110 Philosophy **EQUATION for SUCCESS:**

Clear Vision & 110% Engagement in Life

+

Structure & Discipline

=

HAPPINESS & SUCCESS!

When you consistently apply Structure and Discipline to everything you do, harnessing a precise way of thinking, you will achieve your vision for your life. And that, folks, will make you happy!

The *110 Philosophy* stops and asks these critical questions:

1. **What is my Vision – Where am I going?**

   If you don't have a clear idea of where you are going, you are merely floating along at the mercy of others. How can you possibly make any progress in life if you can't describe your Vision for yourself?!

2. **Am I fully engaged in my life – Am I set up to achieve my Vision?**

   Look, engagement is where it is at! If you are not excited about where you are going (your Vision), then you have the wrong vision! What gets you excited?!

3. **Do I have Structure – What elements or routines do I need to keep me focused?**

There are foundations in life that help keep our priorities in order and our focus on what is really important. Having a structure that sets clear priorities that you value keeps you focused. It also provides a safety net when things go awry – you have something to turn to because you *know* what is important to you.

4. **How do I maintain Discipline – How can I avoid distractions that keep me from my goals?**

Most days, life is one distraction after another. It is way too easy to check out from our lives, our goals and what is really important, and just drift from one drama to another. Before you know it, the day, the week, the year has passed, and nothing has improved! We need to take intentional, disciplined actions in response to all of these distractions or we will derail. Our daily routines, automated responses to challenges, and habits of self-care and decision making can keep us on course.

5. **How's my Life – How do I balance everything and ensure there's time for myself, my friends, and my family?**

Keeping an intentional eye on things that bring the deeper value to life – spirituality, self-care, relationships – impact our lives significantly for the better. You must have priorities set in these areas that are non-negotiable, no matter how crazy life gets.

6. **Is my Career where I want it – How am I moving myself forward professionally?**

Whether you are on a career track, an entrepreneur, a philanthropist, or manage your home and family, consistently doing some form of self-improvement and learning new skills is important to a healthy, happy mind!

When you utilize the *110 Philosophy* consistently – you not only *know* the answers to these questions – but you *like* the answers!

Here's what you will create for yourself with the tools in this book:

1. A **Vision** so you stay on track with your life.

2. A **Structure** to help you make the right decisions based on a balanced quality of life.

3. **Discipline** to help manage and control your thinking so you can quickly recuperate a positive attitude and minimize distractions. You will build skills to make the necessary decisions and choices to make real change in your level of happiness.

4. *Awareness greater than the power of gratitude!* That's right, the *110 Philosophy* takes gratitude one step further – be thankful for your amazing life and happiness, *yes*, and then figure out how to recreate it in an ongoing fashion! Then teach this *110 Philosophy* to those around you…and WE all might just make OUR world a better place for our children!

Walk with purpose!

110 Philosophy

What is Happiness?

The *110 Philosophy* is not about being happy all the time, every day. That would be silly, and you'd stop reading. It's about how to better handle what life throws your way so that you are happy *more of the time*, and when things are not good, circumstances do not wreck you. The *110 Philosophy* teaches you how to manage your thoughts, to remain positive during tough times, work through challenges faster, and to get on with continued momentum toward your vision for yourself. Happiness is a meter – it goes up and down. The trick is to be paying attention, and know that when your meter is not running high enough, it's time to make some changes. YOU have the power to do that in any moment!

The *110 Philosophy* Happiness Meter

What is your happiness temperature?

**Put your focus on your happiness
and you will have more of it!**

I get told all the time that I have such a "positive attitude," and people always want to know how I maintain such a great outlook no matter what life throws at me. What if I told you that I believe, actually I *know*, that we have the ability to limit negative experiences, and recreate good ones? In other words, the ***level of our happiness is very much within our own control***!

Too much of our focus is on what is wrong, what isn't going right, or what we don't have. In the process, we let happy times pass us by! We skim over happy times, as fleeting moments, or worse – as flukes! I also witness people discounting happiness or not even seeking it, using an excuse such as, "I can't be happy until..." or "after I do X, then I'll be happy." How horrible to take happiness for granted! Truth is, when you manage your thinking through a situation, you can intentionally create more happy times – it's all in the *power of your thinking!*

The key to happiness is maintaining a positive attitude as much as possible. Of course, this is much easier said than done! Most "self-help" books and gurus talk about having a positive attitude, but don't often give a ***how***.

The Key to having a positive attitude is to recognize:

1. Nothing is permanent, so don't get so invested in the negative stuff.

2. Every experience has a valuable lesson attached to it, so learn and move on.

3. When we pay attention to what is good and bad, and then take action to either avoid it in the future or recreate it for another time, we are putting ourselves in control over our happiness!

Hey, life can be challenging! What matters is what you do with tough times – let them ruin your whole existence, sucking happiness and joy out of your life and relationships – or change the way you look at what they have to offer, learn from them accordingly, and whenever possible, devise a way to avoid them in the future. Whether it's a serious health issue, a challenge at work, or frustration from being stuck in traffic; the tools and techniques outlined in this book give you a way to control how you think about what is happening to you, and how you will react. The trick is to have a cue that says, "uh-oh, things are off, what's going on?" then analyze the facts (getting away from the feelings), and determine what choices you have in your control. When you have a plan to handle conflicts, and the discipline to analyze the situation – it's powerful! When you have the power to control your reactions, you can control your happiness!

> *"Life isn't about waiting for the storm to pass;*
> *It's about learning to dance in the rain."*

~ Vivian Greene

I believe true happiness comes as a result of the hard times as a matter of fact. The only way to know happiness, and to be grateful, is to have had the opposite – hard times. In 2016, I was finally diagnosed with a rare autoimmune disease, hyperparathyroidism, that (come to find out) I had been suffering with, I believe, since my childhood. Which explains why I was ALWAYS the sick kid! Over the course of the past two decades I had developed 11 different medical diagnoses, including breast cancer and subsequent treatments, as well as a need to have both my feet operated on in 2018. The years leading up to my autoimmune disease diagnosis were some of the most difficult times in my life. Many days I wouldn't say I was happy, but I was deeply aware that I was *alive*. And when some days were better than others, I concentrated on those better days, and looked for ways to repeat them. For example, when my second foot surgery was approaching, I could have been filled with dread, knowing what significant pain, loneliness and boredom was coming. However, because I practice the *110 Philosophy* every day and in every situation, I approached it very differently. Learning from the struggles I could avoid from the first surgery experience, I made sure I had plenty of support on hand to help me. I purchased a shower chair and all new shower products so I could have a better shower experience, because that was one of my only times to be upright – I wanted it enjoyable! I made sure many daily conveniences (electronics, snacks, miniature individual refrigerator) were at arm's length. And, I bought new comfortable clothes so I could enjoy a new outfit, even though I was bedridden.

This is a fundamental part of the *110 Philosophy* – to dissect a situation and to learn from it (what to avoid, what to repeat). In understanding life's up and down cycles, bad days give us an appreciation of good days. Life is about the ***pursuit of happiness***. That is what happiness is all about – it's about the journey, accepting that fact alone will make you a happier person.

Happiness doesn't happen TO you, it happens FOR you.

As promised, here is a great exercise to remind you that happiness is available to you in any moment. **Let me introduce one of the fundamental *110 Philosophy* tools:**

EXERCISE: The Great Day Continuance

I want to be clear early on that the tools and exercises in this book are NOT just about dealing with the negative stuff in life, the struggles and challenges. It is ***just as important*** to pay attention to and analyze the good times! In fact, I believe it is MORE important. After all, that's what we want more of, right?! Well, to recreate the good, we must first understand how it came to be. So this exercise is one that I personally use all the time for myself and with my staff in my business. It takes the time to STOP and analyze what happened that went well or felt good, how it happened, and why it was so good – that way we can replicate it! This exercise doesn't take a lot of time, but is a powerful tool if you want more good in your life.

Consider a recent experience that you felt went really well or made you feel really great. Now let's dig into it a bit:

What made this day/experience good for me?

What happened? Describe the experience or day in detail. Sometimes, using a timeline helps, or go through your activities and how you spent your time, get specific about both your activities and the people involved. What was said or done, who said or did it, how did things unfold?

What does it feel like? Be as specific with your thoughts as you can. What specifically gave you feelings of happiness? What relieved the feelings of stress or sadness? Describe your feelings in detail.

Visualize the experience/day in your mind. Run through the experience once more and work to see it in your mind (closing your eyes helps). Visualization is a powerful tool not only for what you want to happen, but for developing the ability to recreate events.

Once you have figured out what the driving factors are when you experience happiness, the easier it will be to replicate it! You can't do that until you have dissected all the elements of it and analyzed what factors contributed to it, specifically. Now that you know what makes for a great day – REPLICATE IT as much as possible!

For example, most of us don't love Mondays. Admittedly, I am not a fan, mostly because I so enjoy my weekends with my family. I resist getting back at it on Monday as much as anyone! One week I worked from home on Monday. I had my to-do list and my work schedule to keep, but WOW, it was a much more enjoyable day and when Tuesday came around I felt more ready to go to work. Now, I haven't always been able to work from home on Monday, but that experience taught me to work in transition time back to the workweek for myself. So, I have a "rule" that nothing is scheduled on my calendar on Monday mornings between 9:00 a.m. and 11:00 a.m. During this time I now do my bookkeeping, which is a task I have traditionally disliked, but because I have this quiet time blocked off, I get it done. I feel a huge sense of accomplishment, and transition myself better into the workweek. I know this makes me more productive because I have eliminated all the time that resistance costs us in procrastination and other time wasters we do when we are unhappy.

Everyone likes more than just one example, and here's another one – as I use this one a lot when I am coaching my team, family and friends. Did you eat all of the cookies last night? If you did – and now you are feeling terrible about that decision – ask yourself why did you eat all the cookies, when your goal is to wear a pair of jeans? Figure out exactly what was going on – were you tired; were they just plain good; were you sad about something? What could you do differently the next time? How about just eating 5 cookies versus the entire plate? And then compliment yourself by saying, "Good Job Luanne! I only ate 5 rather than the entire plate. Now next time try and only eat 4," etc. You see where I am going with this. Now, what if you only ate 3 to begin with? MAKE SURE you compliment yourself when you really did a great job with discipline. Figure out why this time you could stop with only eating 3 but the last few times you ate the entire plate of cookies. This is key to the success of repeating the positive behavior. You have to stop long enough to actually focus on the positive!

ROCK the mirror – inside and out!

110 Philosophy: STRUCTURE

OK, now it's time to get into the nuts and bolts of the *110 Philosophy*! To experience success at anything, you need to have a framework to support your efforts and changes. You will need to have a way to assess how you are doing with your priorities, time management, and decision-making. All change or success in life comes by having a structure in place to implement your plan. Without structure, even the most decisive actions fall flat because they are not operating within any determined path.

110 Philosophy Structure

Vision – Without a clear vision for where you are going, you are just floundering around through life without a clear direction and commitment to anything. You cannot set clear action goals without a vision for where you are going. Your vision breathes life into your everyday activities!

Engagement – If you are not fully engaged with your vision it will fall flat. Without committed actions you simply won't get anywhere. All this activity that supports your core values and moves you in the direction of your vision is so fun and exciting – it's your reason to get out of bed in the morning!

Guiding Principles – The Guiding Principles set your priorities for your life. They are the values that you adhere to when you make all your decisions, and allow you to determine what is most important when you need to make choices. Having clear priorities makes things so much easier!

The Guiding Principles of the *110 Philosophy*, and developing a clear Vision for yourself, will give you this framework. This Structure will be what you will measure your efforts against. The Guiding Principles give you "policies" for how you will prioritize your time, manage situations, and make decisions. When you are striving to be better, you will trip up, we all do; they also give you a quick way to get yourself back on track.

110 Philosophy Guiding Principles:

1. **Spirituality**
2. **Self**
3. **Spouse/Key Partnership**
4. **Family/Friendships**
5. **Career**

These principles will be explained in more detail in a subsequent chapter.

Structure is essential because it gives you a mechanism in place:

1) to alert you when you are off course;
2) to identify what is not working; and then,
3) to give you tools to adjust your plan and make the necessary adjustments.

The beauty of the *110 Philosophy* gives you not only *what* you need to do, but it gives you the ***how*** to get there – and how to correct when necessary!

Because we want to keep practicing new approaches to life while you are learning the *110 Philosophy* – here is another basic exercise I use all the time. The **110 Basic Tool** is a great way to break a cycle of letting daily aggravations derail your happiness, and put a disciplined way to figure out what to do differently in place instead.

110 Basic Tool

We face challenges every day, some big, some small. I've been held captive to the aggravation of running late to work and letting it ruin my whole morning. I've laid awake at night worrying about my son. I know, however, that those feelings of frustration, anger and fear are simply alert mechanisms. Whether they are simple daily aggravations or big life concerns, the thing that these feelings have in common is the fact that they are important signals.

Alert: I'm not feeling okay, something is wrong!

The *key* is to interrupt these thoughts with a basic problem-solving technique. By dissecting a situation that is bothering you, and by asking specific questions and looking at the facts of what is really going on, we can figure out what needs to change. From there, it's a matter of creating a plan to make the necessary adjustments, the changes necessary to move through this challenge and onto resolution. THAT information is power! That is the basic premise of the *110 Philosophy* – to regain control over your life so you can create the happiness you desire!

EXERCISE: The 110 Basic Tool

Describe the challenge/issue. What's happening – the FACTS:

_____

_____

Why is this happening? Who are the players? Who has ownership? What decision led to this experience?

_____

_____

_____

What needs to change? (time allotted, people involved, expectations)

_____

_____

_____

What have you learned about what is/isn't working? What are your take-aways?

_____

_____

_____

What are potential solutions or changes <u>I can make</u>?

_____

_____

_____

_____

I'm going to share with you how I used this exercise recently in my own life, so you can see how it works:

Describe the challenge/issue. What's happening – the FACTS: <u>Getting the lawn mowed consistently.</u>

It would seem so simple, with two teenagers and a husband, that the lawn could get mowed. But, it was always left off the list for everyone, and I was left frustrated at my ugly lawn, and angry at my housemates. After numerous "fairness" approaches, with a rotation system put into place, then a demand process put into place, nothing was really working. SO, I needed to dissect this problem further.

Why is this happening?

No one but me had pride in a tidy yard on a consistent basis. They just didn't really care, quite frankly. Therefore, I really did own the challenge. Ah ha! The problem wasn't on them, it was on me!

What needs to change?

Because this issue was all about the idea I had in my head, I had to change my mentality – yup, I had to change the way I was thinking of the situation. Instead of demanding that the men in my life take care of the situation that was upsetting me, I had to take care of it for me to achieve the lawn "happiness" I envisioned!

What are potential solutions or changes I can make?

I LOVE a good work out – listening to the tunes and sweating. So, I changed my mentality to viewing the lawn mowing chore as my workout for the day. I crank the tunes and I sing, and alongside a lawnmower I can really crank it out! No need for a gym – I can get out in my own yard for a good workout, achieve the vision for my lawn myself, and no more cranky-pants to my boys!

So you can see, with the *110 Philosophy* at work here, I took a challenging situation, I dissected it to determine what was really wrong or what was the real challenge was, then I was able to figure out how change my mentality to see this situation as a positive situation versus a negative one, and what changes I needed to make. My solution here isn't the only one available, yours might be different. Perhaps you would choose to pay someone to mow the lawn, or you would try another arrangement to get someone to do it – laundry in exchange for mowing…who knows, but the point is until you really understand all the pieces, you can't really resolve something, and that's how we get stuck in stewing, worrying, and resentment over situations.

If you are having a bad day, have a bad day, because tomorrow is a new day!

"Luanne Cameron has been able to take her passionate coaching skills, couple them with the 'new day of small and large business,' and establish a culture in her agency that is truly "WOW" for her team and customers! I had the joy of visiting her office and instantly wanted the same environment for my office. Luanne immediately volunteered to be my coach! Her laser focus, passion, desire to share, and ability to stay on target is exactly what is needed today! I believe she can catapult any agencies to the next level.

Luanne has a *110 Philosophy* that is contagious! It will help you manage your business to success! Businesses small and large can capitalize on her giftedness. She believes in truly helping her community, businesses small and large and her message will resonate with them all!"

~ Dennis Keller Agent, Owner, Keller Insurance Agency (30+ years)

110 Philosophy: STRUCTURE

YOUR VISION – Map your road to happy!

I believe to accomplish anything, you must have a clear Vision. When we set out to do something – land a new job, lose weight, or paint the living room – we have a picture in our mind of what it will look like to sit in that new office, feel great in that new pair of jeans, or wear a new pair of socks, what the couch will look like against the green walls – a vision for the end result. Not having a Vision for yourself is like setting out in your car to go somewhere with no directions, no map; heck, put on a blindfold while you're at it! It makes *no sense!*

The definition[*] of Vision is:

> ## vi-sion
> /'viZHen/
> noun
>
> 1. The faculty or state of being able to see.
>
> 2. The ability to think about or plan the future with imagination or wisdom.
>
> verb
> imagine

* per lexico.com

Having a Vision is about looking toward the future with imagination and wisdom. In business language, a vision is often described as, "an inspirational description of what the organization would like to achieve or accomplish." A Vision is intended to serve as a clear guidepost for all future courses of action. If you are going to take charge of your future (your happiness!), then you must have a Vision to guide you!

Your Vision MUST be engaging. It needs to incite feelings of excitement and something that is fun to work toward. It must really deeply mean something to YOU – there must be a significant, emotional attachment to your Vision. It is not what you think you "should" do in your life, or what someone else tells you would be good for you. A good Vision impacts all areas of life; it is not restricted to what you want from your business, or what you want in your personal life. Zoom out farther if necessary, and consider what really matters to you, what impacts you every day, what will really make you happy. Your Vision is accurate if you can put your priorities, decisions, and planning/goals up against it as a way to decide how you will respond and spend your time.

Your Vision:

- Keep your Vision clear and focused, not vague. "To be happy" is not a Vision. "To be the top dry-cleaning business in the city" is a Vision.

- Your Vision *is not* a goal; goals evolve from our Vision, goals are the steps to get you there.

- Your Vision should make you feel excited and energized!

When my mother left my father and married my dad's best friend, my family was thrown into turmoil. I suddenly went from a stable, happy home life, to living in poverty under the worst of circumstances. I determined right then that I would never live like that as an adult. I would do what whatever was necessary to find the right person to share my life with, create the family I wanted, and build a career that allowed me to create security for myself and my family. Realizing in childhood what I didn't want, gave me the insights at a young age to manage my own future and create the life I did want. This is having a Vision for yourself – awareness of what you want in life for the long-term.

Where did the 110 vision come from? Well, the idea came way back in my childhood. My grandmother was very special in my life. She was one of the only adults that would talk to me about my parents' divorce, and with whom I felt safe. My grandmother ran a nursing home, and so I always had a lot of elders around me. I

79

remember when I was age five, my grandmother introduced me to a man who was 100 years old. It was a big deal for me at the time; I had never met anyone so old. And, I remember going into his room to visit him. After being allowed to speak with him, I remember that I said to myself, "I'm going to live to be 100 years old." So that is where the initial concept came from. Years later, during a conversation with my mother over longevity, we were bantering back and forth about lifespans. She shared with me that we had family members who had lived to be 103 years old. I decided to add a lucky seven years to 103 – and 110 became my new longevity goal! I loved this nice round number, and so it has become my corporation name and my personal philosophy moniker as well!

I'll share both my Personal Vision and my Business Vision with you:

My Personal Vision is: Living happily to be 110 years young.
My Business Vision: To be the office culture model for the country!

Here's the real kicker – it doesn't matter if you actually obtain your Vision! I don't know for sure that I can live to be 110; but, that doesn't matter! What matters is I have that big Vision for myself, and I care about it deeply. My Vision determines how I run my life – all the decisions I make about how I spend my time I put up against my Vision as the litmus test of whether it is a good idea. The same holds true for the business decisions I make – if we do (this) does it support us becoming the best office culture in the country?

I absolutely love the quote from Walt Disney:

"It's kind of fun to do the impossible!"
~ Walt Disney

Walt Disney said this in response to people asking him why in the world he thought he could build a world-famous family theme park in the middle of a swamp in Florida. People thought he was crazy, but he didn't care. *He had a vision.* He kept working at his vision, citing that it was fun to work toward the impossible – and look at Disney World today. He basically has created what was considered impossible! I have a poster of this quote hanging in my office as a reminder to keep this spirit alive. My vision seems impossible, even crazy, to most but it is very doable to me. And I truthfully am not focused on whether I achieve it or not. I focus on 'if I want to achieve that, what do I need to do *now?*' That is why I say your Vision needs to be HUGE, not even attainable perhaps, so it will pull you forward with passion for what you really care about.

A Vision pulls you forward, and gives you a laser focus for your life. Visions are very individual and very personal. Maybe it's where you want to go to work every day, or maybe you want to start your own business, write a book, or have a child. Maybe your Vision is to have a healthy body, or a home you love. Visions are different for everyone. Visions are your optimal desire, providing guidance and inspiration, functioning as your North Star. With a Vision, you can base choices and actions against if it is supporting your Vision or not – see how easy decision-making just got?! You can't implement a Structure in your life for success, and operate with Discipline in what you do, if you don't know where you are going! That is why it is so important to have a Vision!

To create a Vision that will work for you, and stick for the long run, you need to stay very present minded and realistic. This is a process that gets real – focused on what is actually happening, analyze the facts of your life, and then you can determine what can actually be changed.

Other Examples of Vision Statements:

Oprah Winfrey's Vision: *"To be a teacher. And to be known for inspiring my students to be more than they thought they could be."*

Richard Branson's Vision: *"To have fun in [my] journey through life and learn from [my] mistakes."*

Vision and Goals are Different

There is a difference between Vision and Goals, and it's important to distinguish between the two. Vision is where you want to go, your big picture. How you get there – the actions and steps involved – are your goals. Goals support your Vision, but do not replace having your one, big picture for a happy life in your mind!

Your Vision is what will guide you in your daily life, providing the direction necessary to chart your course, to make decisions about everything from daily life matters to big impact decisions. Similar to my poster of Walt Disney's quote, keep your Vision front and center where you can see it, and model it!

Honing YOUR Vision

Developing your Vision is the absolute critical first step to fully incorporating the *110 Philosophy* into your life. Some people reach it quickly, some need more time to think and reflect, but I will suggest you *just do it*. If you wait for just the right time to do this exercise, it will never happen.

You may want to consider having different Vision statements as I do, perhaps a personal one and one if you lead your own business. It is absolutely wonderful to have a business vision that you share with your staff and that everyone can buy into.

Just like I want to be a role model for my children, my family and my friends, I want my business to be a role model. My Vision for my business, remember, is to be a model office for the country. I want this book to be a model for people to follow to help themselves have happier lives. What drives me is to pay it forward – to fulfill a greater purpose with my life. For my own spirituality, I want to be a living testimony of God. I want to be someone God can be proud of for making a difference in other people's lives. That is what drives me – to make others smile! The same factors that will make me push myself to be the best I can be, are the same principles to make my office, my team of leaders, the best they can be. I also believe, you can't run a successful business if you can't run a successful household! So, the importance of knowing your priorities in life is critical to the equation of success/ happiness!

You want a Vision statement that is simple to recall and easily understood especially if you will be sharing it with others (your family, your entire team). I also believe that the more you share your Vision, the clearer it becomes and the more ingrained it will be as a basis for your decision-making. Once you have your Vision Statement, write it down everywhere – post it in your office, on your refrigerator, by your mirror in your bathroom. Set your smart phone wallpaper to it written out. Find quotes that support your Vision and post those too!

To create your Vision, ask yourself these introspective questions to help you pull together your thoughts. You can use this book as a workbook, copy these pages; or, just use a plain notebook, your phone, or sticky pads – I don't care as long as you start doing it! Ultimately, we are going for a fairly simple, concise Vision Statement.

What is your BIG vision for yourself?!

EXERCISE: Vision Statement

For this exercise – get quiet. Take some deep cleansing breaths, and consider each question. I think it is helpful to close your eyes while you consider each question – *visualization* is key to having a vision! Consider these questions, describe each in detail – what does it look, sound, feel, taste like? What do you look like? Really focus on the details, tap into as many senses as you can for each area. Be very honest – your answers can't help you unless you are really truthful!

This mind visual will help you answer these deep questions. Now I'm not a big fan of that 'Write your own eulogy' exercise. So let's try something more positive: Close your eyes, find a quiet spot. Envision you are an elderly version of yourself and you are in your favorite rocking chair on your ideal porch. The sunshine is on your face, and you are looking back on your life up until this very idealistic moment. What does it feel like? Are you satisfied and at peace? What does it look like? Can you see the years before you filled with happy times with loved ones, accomplishment of your biggest goals? Did you fulfill your greatest dreams? What accomplishments did you achieve? What stories are you excited to share with your great grandchildren? What do you want them to know you for?

As this mind visual becomes vivid, think about what 5 things do you most enjoy doing? (Look back on your calendar or think about how you spent your time over the last few months – what gave you the most joy, made time fly by, without which you would feel incomplete?)

I know exactly what I will look like when I am 110 years young. I know what jewelry I will be wearing, what my hair and clothing will look like. And I know I will have enough money in the bank not to worry about paying for my fancy hair cut. AND, I definitely will NOT be in a wheel chair, 125 pounds overweight. It is this exact vision that helps me say "NO" to the freshly baked cookies!

To envision our Personal or Business Visions, we need to set goals using the Guiding Principles.

> ### *110 Philosophy* Guiding Principles:
>
> 1. **Spirituality**
> 2. **Self**
> 3. **Spouse/Key Partnership**
> 4. **Family/Friendships**
> 5. **Career**

Write one important goal (something you want to improve, learn or make a priority) **for each of the 5 Guiding Principles for your life that are in alignment with your happy elderly version of yourself:** (My answers are in the parenthesis.)

1. **Spirituality** (God)

   _____

2. **Self** (Hair)

   _____

3. **Spouse/Key Partnership** (my husband, JP)

   _____

4. **Family/Friends Relationships** (our kids)

   _____

5. **What makes me feel most fulfilled in my Career?**
    (Helping others be their best)

   _____

Additional thought provoking questions:

If I never had to work another day in my life, what would I be doing? _____

How is my financial security? How do I want it to change?

   _____

When do I have the most fun? _____

What are my long-term goals? _____

Where do I see myself in 1, 3, 5, 50 years? _____

110 Philosophy: STRUCTURE

110% Engagement in Your Vision

To embody the *110 Philosophy* you must have full engagement in your Vision! What does that mean? You are truly engaged in something when you feel energy surging through you about it – it's the stuff that keeps us awake at night, ideas that make us jump out of bed in the morning. A feeling of certainty, of conviction.

Your level of excitement and engagement is your litmus test for whether your Vision is right for you. What is the best part about feeling engaged? It's FUN! Feeling excitement, having energy to put into something – that is what fun is. Your **110% Engagement** in your **Vision** is what gets you out of bed every morning, ready to tackle the day because you have a bigger picture in your mind.

Once I was clear about my Vision for myself – to live to be a healthy, active 110 years young – I knew I would have to be **110% Engaged** in my life, every day, to achieve that. I don't want to just tick away the days; I want every day to count and be enjoyable. What would that involve? Well, I would need to take really good care of my health – regular checkups, good nutrition, and exercise. I would need to have healthy relationships, because we know dysfunctional relationships can cause tremendous stress, and stress kills. I would need a career that was fulfilling (back to stress killing again), and that career better be enjoyable every day! I wasn't going to jump out of bed, do my hair and makeup every day, and put my kids in daycare, if I wasn't going to enjoy it! Finally, I would need to have the resources to support myself for another 55 years, because being old and poor doesn't sound like a good time. That pretty much gave me my roadmap to reach my vision.

Now feeling this excitement, this commitment, an *engagement* in my Vision, doesn't mean I feel this way every second of every day. However, when there are actions I need to take to achieve my vision – say, going to an unpleasant medical test (because, remember, to live to 110 I need to take good care of myself!), what propels me to do this unpleasant effort *is* my engagement. The commitment to my Vision (engagement in it) propels me forward through things I would rather avoid or procrastinate about. I never *wanted* to go to my mammogram that day, but my Vision to live to 110 means that I go to all the necessary preventative screenings and tests! When breast cancer was discovered, it shook me to my core of course, but I had my vision. I am 110% engaged in my health in order to support my Vision, and so I dealt with it as I needed to. I realigned my priorities, and faced it head on. While it certainly wasn't an enjoyable journey for me, imagine if I hadn't gone to that mammogram! The methods of the *110 Philosophy* truly work in all situations.

True 110% Engagement is a belief in your Vision – in yourself – so strong that it propels you into action, no matter what!

To ensure you are supporting the *110 Philosophy* Structure, it is important to have ongoing reviews and to check-in with yourself. There are so many ways that I jumpstart my 110% Engagement every day to keep it on top of my mind and in support of my bigger picture – my Vision. My favorite daily exercises are short (take only a few minutes) and sweet (what's sweeter than a positive focus on your own happiness?!).

My typical "110 Day" looks something like this:

- I get up early enough so that I have time to get ready for work, or whatever I am doing, without feeling rushed. Starting your day off in a frantic rush is a huge mistake!

- I stretch and get my body engaged and woken up. I never hit the snooze button! Note: I know I get enough sleep if I wake up before my alarm goes off. If the alarm wakes me, I make a mental note to get more sleep the next night.

- Once I'm out of bed, I drink a large glass of water. This is followed by a shot of apple cider vinegar, and then another large glass of water before I'm out the bedroom door.

- Shower time is my thinking time, so it's a very important time for me. I often play what I consider positive music while I'm getting ready.

- I give myself plenty of time to do hair and makeup, and get out the door prepared. I have them timed out so I keep my eye on the clock, and stick to my routine.

- I eat a couple of eggs or a simple breakfast so I'm out the door with some sustenance in my body.

- On my commute I listen to positive talk radio, and it's more time for thinking.

- When I get to work, my morning is already planned out. By lunchtime, I'm looking ahead to see how tomorrow is shaping up, and by 4:00 p.m. I'm making sure tomorrow is in good shape and there are no loose ends. Note, by midweek I'm looking out to the rest of the week to make sure everything is confirmed and organized, and by week's end I'm looking into the next week. I like to head off surprises – it's much easier to resolve challenges when you can see them coming! I have a lot of structure around my business operations, but that's a practice anyone can incorporate into their workday.

- Ending the day on time at 5:00 p.m. is important to me and my team. We work very hard during the day, but whenever possible we are out the door on time!

- I set aside time to work out several times a week. This is key to my Vision for a healthy life at 110.

- My favorite dinner is "FFY" – which is "fend for yourself"! After that, it's time to relax as I believe there needs to be time each day for downtime.

- Before the end of the day I prepare for the next day. I plan my outfit, do any ironing or food preparation I need for the next day, and make sure I am ready for tomorrow's schedule. I do this before I put on my PJ's because I feel I am still in "work mode" a bit so I'm better at these tasks in that state of mind.

EXERCISES for 110% Engagement:

➢ **Set My 110 for the Day** (daily intention-setting)

➢ **Daily Diagnosis** (habit of reviewing how the day went)

➢ **Rituals** (morning rituals, before bed rituals, affirmations)

➢ **Reminders** (mirror/stickie notes posts, quotes, pictures)

➢ **Opportunity to Refresh** (reset focus when things go off track, set goals based on occasions like birthday, holidays)

A great hair day is an awesome day!

When I'm anxious about an upcoming event, I post reminders to encourage myself.

I made this acronym with my name to help me remember what I want to be working on.

When I had debilitating foot surgery, I put my dancing boots right where I could see them to remind me I would be up on my feet and dancing one day!

These exercises are covered in detail in the next few pages, and really begin to bring the *110 Philosophy* all together. These active, daily 110% Engagement activities and exercises support the structure of the Guiding Principles and your Vision, and provide the action steps of the Discipline that is required to truly take charge of your attitude, your reactions, and your life – in other words, your HAPPINESS!

Work HARD, play HARD!

"I have known Luanne both professionally and personally for 15 years, and have always been impressed by her focus and dedication to both her business and what is important in her life overall. Her philosophy of always giving 110% to everything she does is an inspiration! Having worked in her office as an intern, I was especially impressed by the culture she has built of respect, dedication to results, and excellent customer service. I believe Luanne is such a success because she has a clear vision, a focus on her goals, and a discipline to sustain her efforts long-term. I know firsthand that her team and her customers appreciate her 110% commitment to providing a remarkable experience."

~ Judy Lamoureux, Insurance Agency Field Specialist, Trainer

110 Philosophy: STRUCTURE

The Guiding Principles

The **Guiding Principles** of the *110 Philosophy* are the foundation of the methodology. They are the fundamental **Structure** that provides the necessary attention to key areas of your life, from which you will base your daily decision-making. Using the **Guiding Principles** consistently provides the awareness to alert us when things are out of balance in our lives; gives us the ability to retain laser focus on what is important; and helps us to minimize distractions that take us off course.

I realized I needed to adjust my priorities when I was working 80 hours a week in my corporate job and traveling all the time. I thought, "What am I doing with my life, where am I going with my family and career, where do I *want* to go?!" Then I dug deep; I worked hard to picture in my mind what my life was going to look like, feel like, and even smell like when I got there. What did I look like? I envisioned my clothes, my hair. What car did I drive to work? I pictured the car in my driveway. What did my house look like? By answering these few basics questions it became clear what mattered to me, and what would most greatly impact my personal happiness. I always knew I intended to live a long time, so this was my direction – longevity! I now had a clear Vision of where I wanted to go (to live to be 110). So, then I needed to create the habits and decisions by building Structure and Discipline into my life to get there.

I have come to call these priorities the **Guiding Principles** of the *110 Philosophy*. Each one of these principles has been tested over the course of several decades, and the order of priority for them is VERY clear to me. Every time I didn't have them in the right order – I found myself unhappy.

What I have learned through life's most challenging moments is that decisions are easier to make when my Vision is clear, which makes my priorities easier for me to determine, and I hold fast to them (no exceptions!). For example, getting back to my Vision to live to be a healthy, vibrant 110-year-old; if that is my Vision, then I need Discipline with my life choices that support it. You might be figuring out by now that I love cookies, and I could eat a lot of them. But, that does not support my health priorities (which support that greater Vision), so I limit my intake of sweets.

It is so easy to "eat the cookie." Of course, sometimes I eat cookies, and sometimes too much; I'm human. Now, I could beat myself up and fall apart altogether in my nutrition; or I can just accept I ate too many sweets and move on to tomorrow. The key is that after I falter, I always analyze why. Have I been too strict in my diet? Am I not addressing a stressor in my life? Figure out what is going on; then you can make plans for how to handle things better in the future. So the next time, maybe I only eat two cookies. Hey, I could have eaten the whole platter, so this is something to congratulate myself for. The important thing is to get back up, learn from it and move on. That is what I hope the Guiding Principles will do for you.

These key areas of life impact your effectiveness. When we ignore one area in favor of another, too much and too often, our lives and work suffer. Your ability to be happy in your life, and be a successful leader, depends on **managing balance among these critical aspects of your life in <u>this order of priority</u>**:

110 Philosophy **Guiding Principles:**

1. **Spirituality**
2. **Self**
3. **Spouse/Key Partnership**
4. **Family/Friendships**
5. **Career**

The Guiding Principles are the foundation that the *110 Philosophy* is built on – you must pay attention to each one of these areas of your life, ***in the order of priority that they are outlined***, to have a balance that can sustain your energy, your focus, and consequently, your happiness. We already have each one of these areas at work in our lives now. They each exist in the cosmos. We just may be ignoring or discounting some of them in our other pursuits (mistakenly thinking they do not matter). When you don't get enough rest or don't take good care of yourself, you get sick. When you ignore a relationship, whether it's date night with your spouse or brunch with your friends, eventually that relationship will go away, dying from neglect and lack of respect.

These key areas of life impact your effectiveness. When we ignore one area over another, our lives and work suffer.

Back to my time of working 80 hours a week and juggling a crazy schedule. I would work until 3:00 a.m. to get my work done, so I wouldn't miss time with my kids. I was willing to work hard during the week in order to have time on the weekends to spend with my family. My decision was based on my Guiding Principles of putting family before career. At one point in my corporate career, my Vice President told me that everyone was going to have to work Saturdays in order to get our workload done. I held strong to my priorities, stating that we needed flexibility. People could choose to work Saturdays, or they could choose to work late nights. The goal was to get the work done, but I wanted everyone to have flexibility in how we got there. I'm proud I held to my convictions, and because I had a clear Vision and my Guiding Principles established for myself, I could stand strong and confident in my decisions!

110 Philosophy Guiding Principles:

 1. **Spirituality**

    2. Self

    3. Spouse/Key Partnership

    4. Family/Friendships

    5. Career

Guiding Principle # 1: Spirituality

How each one of us connects to our spirituality is deeply personal, and I want to be very clear that I am not talking about your religious beliefs. Spirituality in the context of the *110 Philosophy* is about connecting to something that is greater than the material/physical here-and-now. It is where we find our hope, our sense of purpose and how we contribute as human beings. We can't control everything that happens to us, and this is a source of pain for many. How do you go about life knowing this, and not feel helpless, hopeless? When we feel victimized by life, like there is no point or we have no purpose, we are disconnected from our Spirituality. But when you have some sense of faith, you have the inner strength to forge on, knowing that things will work out, that everything will be okay, that there is a greater plan.

While we can't control everything that happens to us, we can control our thinking about it. We *always* have control over our thoughts! Building a strong inner-self (our spirit) is key to getting through tough times.

I personally identify with Christianity and believe in and pray to God. Shortly before my parents divorced, they became very religious, joining a very dogmatic church. The church's practices were forced on me; however, I chose a different path of religion.

Their idea of spirituality wasn't for me. My decision was not to turn away from God, but to embrace the importance of Spirituality in my life. My relationship with God reminds me to be true to myself, true to my family, good to others, and work to teach others how to live more fully. I never want to "preach" to anyone, I'm simply suggesting that our higher purpose, our Spirituality or relationship to the God of our choice, provides a foundation on how we live our lives, set our priorities, and make good choices for ourselves.

I don't believe it matters what higher power or higher consciousness you believe in. I do believe that we need to believe in *something* outside of ourselves and our current physical being. I personally found hope through my cancer diagnosis and treatment by connecting as deeply as I could with my sense of purpose. I know I have a message to deliver, to help others feel better about their lives, to take charge of their own happiness. Because I had to deal so dramatically with my physical self during my treatment and recovery, I feel more confident now, more beautiful. For me, there absolutely was *good* that came out of my cancer. I found a much deeper connection to my spirit and my purpose. This gives meaning to my life, meaning for why bad things happen.

EXERCISE: How do you connect to your Spirituality?

Spirituality is a deeply personal practice. For some, it is going to formal religious services, for others it is meditation, journaling, taking time in nature to reflect. Describe how you take time to connect with your spirit and the deeper meaning of life:

_____

_____

_____

_____

_____

_____

_____

110 Philosophy Guiding Principles:

1. Spirituality
☞ 2. **Self**
3. Spouse/Key Partnership
4. Family/Friendships
5. Career

Guiding Principle # 2: Self

We've all heard the saying, "You can't pour from an empty vessel." You are no good to anyone if you don't take care of yourself. What that means to you is different than to someone else, but there are basics we can agree on: eat well, get good sleep, exercise regularly, and go to doctors for checkups. I'd add to this to keep yourself together (get a haircut, wear clean clothes that fit). If you run around looking like a mess, how can you feel good about yourself and have confidence? When I was sick, on days I felt down, I would force myself to get out of bed and get dressed. It always made me feel better – more human! Do things that make you feel good, and *good about yourself.* I do believe that our outsides reflect our insides!

I'm not only talking about outer beauty. You must have love for yourself on the inside too! You can't possibly truly love others if you don't love yourself first. Nothing outside of ourselves can make us feel good – not a spouse, kids, friends, or your career can make you happy if you don't love yourself. Look in a mirror and really look at yourself every day. Consider how you feel about yourself, change the things you do not like, tell yourself out loud what you love and appreciate about yourself.

To totally love who you are, you have to be honest about your weaknesses, your strengths, and accept them fully. Or work to change them if it's important to you. I believe in the power of feedback. When I was in the 8th grade, I asked my girlfriends to be brutally honest with me about what they liked and disliked about me. Like 14-year-old girls, they were very honest! While some of what they said at the time did hurt my feelings, I also took much of it to heart and set about changing the negative characteristics such as "being too bossy." I still believe constructive feedback is extremely helpful. Seeing yourself through another's eyes is a powerful exercise. We do this in corporate leadership all the time in performance reviews, peer assessments, and customer feedback programs. Why not take the initiative to ask your closest friends for their candid feedback to help make you more aware of your personality quirks? Remember, it's just feedback – you have the right to accept or reject anything you choose!

Another great exercise is to consider the individuals that you really admire. Watch how they speak, behave, handle situations, and emulate them. Having role models throughout our lives can be incredibly instructive to our behavior.

110 Philosophy Guiding Principles:

1. Spirituality
2. Self
☛ **3. Spouse/Key Partnership**
4. Family/Friendships
5. Career

Guiding Principle # 3: Spouse/Key Partnership

After you have a spiritual relationship established for your soul, and you learn to love and care for yourself, then you can really love someone else. We are social beings and having a significant other with whom to share the ups and downs of life is a pretty fundamental human experience. I'm not saying you aren't complete until you have a love partner. I'm saying if you have a spouse or love partner that relationship should be a top priority to you, after your relationship with your Spirit and the one you have with yourself. Coveting and nurturing this relationship is critical to your overall well-being, so as you make decisions about what is important to you and what you will put your energy into, this person is up at the top.

I believe strongly (and sometimes unpopularly) that this spouse/partner relationship must come before the one with our children. Why? Because our children cannot be truly happy if their parents are not happy together and working cohesively, in a loving relationship. When we choose a spouse, a life-partner, we need to commit to that relationship as the most important relationship outside of ourselves. Your spouse should be your first priority, even before your children. That doesn't mean you don't love and cherish your children – it means you love them enough to model healthy relationships. It also prevents you from raising self-centered children, who think the universe revolves around them (because some day they will discover it does not). The deepest love you can show your children is how loving adult relationships work. And, if you don't put your partner first, you are showing them that partnerships don't really matter. Your spouse will respond accordingly – by putting you first, because that is the cornerstone of the relationship. Furthermore, your children will grow up, become independent, and go on with their independent adult lives. You and your spouse will be back to the two of you, and if you have not been nurturing that relationship right along, you are in for trouble!

If you are not together with the parent of your children, it is still important to find a way to work together regarding your parenting. Divorce has a negative impact on the children involved. Even when it is ultimately the best thing (I don't believe it is healthy to stay in a bad relationship "for the children"), it still means uprooting their living arrangements, their routines, family traditions, etc. If you add feuding parents, the stress on children is considerable, and not fair to them.

My husband is not particularly romantic; it's just not his thing (he's my soulmate, but I didn't say he was perfect!). However, romance is a huge need of mine. It is part of my Vision to have a strong, romantic relationship. So we talked about our relationship and added some Structure to it so romance would become a priority, since it wasn't going to be something he thought of on his own. Each month, we would alternate one of us planning a surprise activity of some kind together. We decided together that we would plan an activity once a month versus every week because we didn't want it to feel like work or pressure. This schedule felt realistic to balance with our other responsibilities, and allow time for each of us to plan something special when it was our turn. One month it was a wonderful picnic lunch at a local lighthouse, some months it was a nice dinner out at a restaurant we hadn't tried before. The important part is that we talked about it, identified our shared Vision, and we put some accountability into both of us engaging in our relationship in a fair way.

Dare to be different!

> ### 110 Philosophy Guiding Principles:
>
> 1. Spirituality
> 2. Self
> 3. Spouse/Key Partnership
> 👉 **4. Family/Friendships**
> 5. Career

Guiding Principle # 4: Family/Friendships

The rest of your relationships are next in priority. They should not come before the previous three – you need a strong center (spirituality), a healthy commitment to yourself (self-care), and, if applicable, a focus on your key love relationship. Friends or other family members should never take priority over your needs, your spouse, or your kids. However, we must have deep, meaningful relationships to be happy, to feel a sense of belonging for a healthy psyche. When we feel isolated, all challenges and issues in life get bigger because we are lacking a good support system. Be sure you are making it a priority to make time for your other relationships – your spouse, children and work will survive a Sunday morning without you while you visit with friends over brunch or take a walk! Speaking of walking – why not kill two birds with one stone? Combine your self-care activities (exercise, getting a massage) by visiting with friends and family!

Dealing with Conflict in Relationships

In any relationship we have the likelihood for disagreements and strife. Sometimes, when it comes to close relationships such as family, we must find a way to deal with a difficult person or situation. Sometimes, we just need to find a way to "get through it," but do so without compromising ourselves. We need to interrupt dwelling on the negative; that is a fundamental principle of the *110 Philosophy*. There is nothing like a tumultuous, difficult relationship to send us down the rabbit hole of dwelling on bad memories, resentment, and hurt. One of my favorite *110 Philosophy* techniques is an exercise I call, **Shelf It!**

My mother passed away just before Christmas in 2018. We had a very challenging relationship during my adult years. Quite frankly, relating to her always brought up old disappointments, and our personalities just didn't mesh well. So what was I to do? I visualized putting all those negative feelings, old resentments, and bad memories of my childhood in a box and visualized putting that box away, high on a shelf. This allowed me to mentally get away from those negative emotions. Seeing my mother, especially in her older years, was important to me. I didn't feel okay about abandoning the relationship, yet I needed to deal with it in a way that was not negative and miserable for both of us.

I wanted to be fully engaged with her when I was talking to her on the phone or visiting with her. My mother was very guilt stricken from the life she had given me and often lamented to me about these feelings. So, when we visited, I would imagine myself taking the box off the shelf that had been placed there from the last time we talked and "opening" the emotional box so I could be present with her and her guilt and emotions about our relationship.

After our conversations, I would take a few moments to breathe, sometimes talk about what had been said with my husband about what had been said, and then I would visualize closing the box and put it back away up on the shelf. When you are dealing with things that are traumatic or negative you have to face them from time to time. It's very important that you do face them, but you don't have to sit with them endlessly.

Have a really strong visual of putting these feelings away – really see yourself putting them away like paperwork. Perhaps they are in file folders by subject (divorce, moving, death of a loved one), putting a tight lid on that box, walking it over to the closet and stretching to put it up high on the top shelf. Close the door and give yourself a break from those difficult experiences!

What I love about the **Shelf It!** exercise is that it does not indulge denial and just ignore something like it doesn't exist (or, worse, that it will go away). It really accommodates difficult feelings and experiences, and gives you a way to set them aside.

EXERCISE: Shelf It!

What is the one thing / feeling that you need to SHELF:

_____

Take the feelings or experiences individually and write specifically what you are feeling:

_____

_____

Just checking in – did you notice that you're on page 55? Are you counting down the pages? Have you noticed that we have changed the title header to reflect my *110 phil0sophy* font? The new style logo is to help you think entirely different about the process.

Can you see the 110 within the word *phil0sophy*? My hope is to encourage you to envision 110 everywhere and to make the *110 phil0sophy* a part of your life.

110 Philosophy Guiding Principles:

1. Spirituality
2. Self
3. Spouse/Key Partnership
4. Family/Friendships

☞ **5. Career**

Guiding Principle # 5: Career

A career is an essential part of our complete package of a happy life – it gives us purpose, financial security, knowledge and growth. The "job" of raising a family or committed volunteer work in your community is certainly included here. But, all the money in the world doesn't matter if your relationships are not functioning well. If your career is consuming everything, over your self-care and your relationships, your life is not at all balanced. This is why Career is the last priority of the Guiding Principles because it will never give you complete fulfillment and happiness without the other principles.

Career is last and doesn't replace ANYTHING else on the Guiding Principles scale – a job, a career, or a vocational calling is not a top priority because you are replaceable! Certainly, you should care about your job and work hard, but NOT at the expense of more important parts of your life. Entrepreneurs are often quick to chime in when I speak about this area, saying, "But I AM my business! It's not that simple for me!" Actually, running your own business is a great example of the need for good balance! When you "are the business" there is nowhere to hide, no boss or other team members to hide behind. Owning your own business requires you to be in tip-top shape, probably more than any other job! If you are depleted, miserable in your relationships, how can you possibly give the best to your customers?! For these very good reasons, even your work in your own business falls after your focus on the other Guiding Principles.

When I was working in my corporate career, I put everything about that job first, working 80 hours a week and traveling much of every month. I never wanted my kids to feel my absence so I worked late into the nights. I was exhausted and miserable, and I knew my life was way out of balance. I finally realized that this was not okay! While my career is very important to me, and I get a lot of satisfaction in my success, what did my life really mean if I was running myself ragged all the time?! I wanted more than a job, and I wanted a job that made me want to jump out of bed in the morning, and one that stimulated and challenged me. I really focused on what I wanted my work to *feel* like. What would my day look like? What would I be doing? Would I be managing people or working independently? Using the *110 phil0sophy*, as you can see, is all about utilizing visualization to help you grasp what you really want, and how you want your life to be.

Along with job satisfaction, I also wanted to make a good living so I would never have to experience the financial issues I lived through as a child in poverty. Remember, part of my vision is to *never* live like that again! So when I was planning my career Vision, a good salary had to be part of that and I planned accordingly. I don't mind hard work; it just needs to satisfy my vision for my life!

The Guiding Principles are so important because they impact everything.

Each of us already has a set of values in our life – so make sure yours are good ones! Good for your spiritual, mental and physical health, good for your relationships, and good for your work life! Our values determine our behavior, ultimately. What we believe is important impacts our attitude and attitude drives our behaviors!

So many people struggle with finding meaning in their life. You've got to have a structure of (good) values in your life because you take that out into the world. Imagine if your life was full and happy because you had a clear set of values that you held in the right order of priority. Imagine if that happiness, because you go about your days satisfied with your choices and behaviors, radiated from you shown in the way you treated people and how you interacted in the world. Bringing a positive attitude, having an overall spirit of happiness – what could have a greater purpose for living than that?!

It's all about what is important to you
and making a plan to have it.

EXERCISE: Guiding Principles Balance Fill-In

The Guiding Principles represent the 5 key areas of our lives, with Spirituality being top priority, and so forth down to our Career/Vocation being lesser priority.

Consider each of these areas in your own life, circle your satisfaction level, indicating how satisfied/balanced you feel for each Principle – 10 being the most satisfied!

Guiding Principles	Satisfaction Level
Spirituality	1 2 3 4 5 6 7 8 9 10
Self	1 2 3 4 5 6 7 8 9 10
Spouse/Key Partnership	1 2 3 4 5 6 7 8 9 10
Family/Friendships	1 2 3 4 5 6 7 8 9 10
Career/Vocation	1 2 3 4 5 6 7 8 9 10

**If you don't use it
you lose it!**

The Guiding Principles: Summary

The **Guiding Principles** are the check-and-balance system from which you will answer critical questions:

- How am I doing? Am I happy? Do I have positive energy?

- Did (that experience) make me feel good or bad? Am I energized or drained?

- What is going on? What is out of whack?

- What needs to change?

- What area am I spending too much/too little time and energy on?

- Do regular check-in, self-check; go through all 5 Guiding Principles; how am I doing? What is going well? What needs adjustment?

These priorities are such a powerful gauge in your life, trust me, you will use them all the time, from whether you will return a phone call now or later, to whether you will apply for a job or break up with your significant other. Once you use this funda-mental checks and balance structure to assess your life-balance, the more second nature they become. Things that steal your time and energy now, things you spend way too much time on, will no longer even register to you as something to pay attention to or spend precious time on. You will get time back in your life – well spent time!

Do NOT make decisions that compromise the priorities set by the Guiding Principles!

Make sure you are not making life decisions compromising those priorities. Sure, sometimes your career is all consuming, or you have a sick child at home needing your undivided attention. But realize that true happiness is when things are more in balance and not compromising other areas.

50

OK! With the structure of the **Guiding Principles** in place, now all you need are good tools and devices to keep you disciplined in your pursuit of your Vision – you are ready to launch into implementing the *110 phil0sophy* in your life!

If you are not growing,

you are dying...

110 phil0sophy

Structure & Discipline

So where are we in this journey through the *110 phil0sophy*? We are about to merge it all together – our clearly defined Vision gives us that big picture of where we want to go, and our daily routine of **110% Engagement** in our values and Vision keep us motivated and enjoying the ride. We know we need the Structure of the Guiding Principles to help us with setting and clarifying our priorities. I think this is a good place to revisit the *110 phil0sophy* **Equation for Success**:

Clear Vision & 110% Engagement in Life

+

Structure & Discipline

=

HAPPINESS & SUCCESS!

When you consistently apply a Structure and Discipline to everything you do, harnessing a precise way of thinking, you will achieve your Vision for your life. All the exercises in this book will help you to consistently apply this Structure and Discipline to your daily life. Here are some more exercises to help you keep your engagement in this new 110 lifestyle of yours going.

EXERCISES for 110% Engagement

"If you don't choose your habits, your habits will choose you."

One of the key components of the *110 phil0sophy* is consistent practicing of the 110 methods. I have been practicing these exercises for years, and I know they work. Once you use the exercises of the *110 phil0sophy* in your daily practice, they will become engrained and simply part of your daily habits. They take very little time (no more time than complaining!), and will have a positive impact on your life – I guarantee! When you pay attention to your thoughts and how you are thinking about your experiences, you have the opportunity to change the way you are interpreting life as it happens. You also have the amazing opportunity to turn negative things around before they get the best of you.

"The secret of your future is hidden in your daily routine."

EXERCISE: Set My 110 for the Day

Your thoughts when you first wake up are critical in determining what kind of day you will have. Setting a positive intention first-thing can change your whole day. I think setting a daily intention as soon as I wake up is key to keeping myself 110% engaged in my Vision and clear on my Guiding Principles! Sometimes this is a simple statement such as, "I intend to drink 110 ounces of water today" or "I will look everyone I encounter in the eye today and say hello."

Here are some other possibilities for daily 110 intentions:

Any old day:

- I intend to exercise 60 minutes today.

- I intend to plan tomorrow's outfits and my lunch for work tonight so my morning is calmer.

When you are anxious:

- I will take time to breathe and pray today.

- I will get through this, this situation is only temporary – this too shall pass.

- I will listen to positive music on my way to/from work.

- I will spend 60 minutes working on (whatever is stressing you out, action is calming).

When you are angry:

- I will keep the end goal in mind and not get stuck in the minutia.

- I want a life-long marriage; this is a small issue (when angry at spouse).

- I will take a time-out to get the facts straight, think through my response and calm down before I respond.

On special occasions:

- I will stay present and appreciate every moment of this day.

- I will see the beauty in this day.

EXERCISE: Daily Diagnosis

Make a habit of reviewing how your day went. Really make a point of doing this every day until it becomes a habit. Do not underestimate the value in reflecting on what you *learned*! Both the things that you did well and the areas where you need improvement teach you so much and help you set your priorities. Things you have done well today – make a habit to note them so you can remember to keep doing things that way! Things you need to improve upon – help you clarify what goals you need to set for learning and skill-building.

Journaling down your answers will really help you, especially in the beginning. You can simply circle or highlight things you need to work on. Once you are a pro, this is a great mental exercise during your commute home from work, while you are cooking dinner, or during your workout.

What went well today?

_____

_____

What could have been improved on?

_____

_____

What would I do differently if I had a do-over?

_____

_____

What did I learn?

_____

_____

EXERCISE: 110 Rituals

If you haven't noticed already, I love rituals! I have a set of morning rituals, before bed rituals, and daily affirmations that I use to start my day off in the most positive way. See page 70 for examples of some of my favorites, and an outline of my typical 110 day. Rituals are a great way to put actions behind your values with set activities you do to remind yourself of your Vision and what is most important to you. It's also a great discipline to help you keep up your positive mindset and behavior changes!

EXERCISE: Reminders

Visual reminders – little notes, posters and pictures, quotes – are very powerful visuals that can immediately remind you of your priorities. I love to post encouragement or things I need reminding of on the mirror in my bathroom so I see it first thing when I get up to wash my face. And it's the last thing I see as I brush my teeth before bed. Our family vacations are always such special times to me, so I always keep small momentos around my sitting and work areas to remind me of our great times as a family or things that hold special meaning to me. Use sticky notes, print quotes, post pictures, or display trinkets that remind you of your Vision, give you encouragement when you need it, things that make you happy or feel positive, and items that just remind you that life is beautiful.

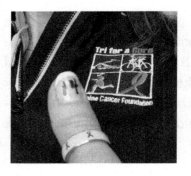

When I'm training for the Tri for a Cure, I write the number of weeks left of training on my thumbnail, to keep a reminder in sight all the time. This is the same thumb I wear my breast cancer survivor ring on which is my daily reminder of what I have lived through to keep me strong when daily challenges test me.

Consistency = SUCCESS!

"In every job that must be done, there is an element of fun. You find the fun and the job's a game."
~ Mary Poppins

EXERCISE: Opportunity to Refresh

As I said, the *110 phil0sophy* is *not* about being blissfully happy every minute of every day. That is completely unrealistic. The best intentions can fail, some days are crappy; people hurt us and make us angry. What you *can* do is give yourself the opportunity to reset your focus when things go off track so that unhappy or bad times don't consume you and derail you for the next month.

I'm a big fan of New Year's Resolutions, new month (heck, new week) resolutions, and goals based on occasions such as birthdays or holidays. I think these significant calendar events are great to mark new beginnings, deadlines or dates to take action! Why not?! Sign up for a road race or buy tickets to an event or a destination, then set your plan for what you need to accomplish to get there. I always have something I want to accomplish by my birthday. When I find I have gained some "holiday weight," I set a goal to have it lost by my birthday four months later. I want to feel great on my birthday, so why not use the time leading up to it to accomplish a goal for myself?

Since my cancer diagnosis I have participated in the Tri for a Cure each year. The training and preparation to have that be a fun and successful experience is no joke! But I love that it is a defined date to work toward as I plan my weekend bike rides and weekday swims and runs. I keep myself energized for training with reminders everywhere (like my thumb countdown), and I buy new, pink training clothes to keep it fun.

Don't beat yourself up. There are enough other people to do that for you!

110 phil0sophy: **DISCIPLINE**

Only when we are consistent with our efforts can real change occur. Putting the *110 phil0sophy* into action is all about Discipline. To be consistent you must be disciplined, but boy that is difficult! Daily demands from our families, friends and jobs, distractions (both good and counter-productive) by things we would rather be doing or escape in, and expectations that buck up against our priorities, all take us away from our focus in any given moment. It's tough to challenge the norms of how we are "supposed" to act, and to separate our feelings from focused thinking in stressful situations. Fear not, I've got you!

Having Discipline:

- **Creates consistency**

- **Holds you accountable**

- **Gives you techniques for responding to life-circumstances**

- **Interrupts panic reactions with planned responses**

One problem is that as humans we are natural rebels. When we are told what to do, we want to do the opposite. Even when it is self-imposed, many people consistently break their promises to themselves, simply because they feel "told what to do" or constricted. This immaturity is one of the main reasons so many people are stuck! My concept of discipline puts a halt to that by interrupting the cycle of bargaining and negotiating with ourselves, with a technique to redirect your thinking. No more going round and round in your head! STOP that cycle and DO something!

Distractions are kept to a minimum because you have a plan ahead of time for handling things that pull your attention away when they come along (because they will!). With the foundation of Structure via your Guiding Principles and a clear Vision guiding you, all you need now is Discipline engrained into your daily actions and reactions to keep you moving steadily in the right direction. *Disciplined responses* will be there to call on when you need to adjust. The exercises already covered in this book give you great daily habits that will help you start your day in a positive, intentional direction; so start using them! Coming up are more exercises to utilize specifically for decision making and problem solving.

We are having an experience in every moment of every day, and how that experience impacts our happiness is 110% in our control! The techniques and tools of the *110 phil0sophy* will guide you through challenging circumstances, so that when something happens to bring you down or throw you off your priorities, you have an immediate resource to refocus. The *110 phil0sophy* is a disciplined way of thinking, using critical analysis (dissecting) of situations with regard to what went well, what needs improvement, and how to adjust your approach in the future.

This is why when you are setting your Vision for yourself you must really see it, feel it, taste it, smell it, be able to define your Vision with all your senses. THAT is what will pull you through on your toughest days. Believe me, when I was recovering from my breast cancer, my hyperparathyroidism neck surgery, my foot surgeries (remember, I had 7 surgeries over the course of 4 years!), the last thing I wanted to do many days was my stretching and strengthening exercises! But it was my clear Vision for my future, a long-term plan, that made me disciplined with my thoughts (not letting myself talk my way out of or rationalize why I didn't need to) so that I could be disciplined with my routine. Reminding myself that I intended to live to be 110 years young meant I did my strengthening routines day after day. Now, when I did miss a day (I'm still human!), I didn't beat myself up about it, but I did set my intention to get back on it tomorrow.

**It boils down to *controlling your thinking*,
and you can learn to do this!**

Controlling Our Thinking

We're unhappy because on some level we are not satisfied in our lives – we are living an unhealthy lifestyle, we are in dysfunctional relationships, we are unfulfilled in our work. It's so easy to get caught up in wallowing in this unhappiness – I call it the "Poor Me Syndrome" – and it's a victim-mentality that says we have no control over our lives. Well sorry (not sorry), but you have more control over your life than anyone else! The *110 phil0sophy* gives you a clear path to take charge of your life in an instant, to pull yourself out of "victim mindset" and put yourself in "power mindset" instantaneously. Doesn't that sound good?!

"Poor Me" Mindset

We have been taught to wait to look for the answers *outside* of ourselves. This is being a victim – saying the world happens *to us*. Well I say the world happens *for us* – we just need to claim our power back! Challenge yourself to really ask, *"Do I like being a victim because it is comfortable here? I don't need to take any risks."* This is very true for some people. You must get out of your comfort zone to make real changes in your life. Even positive change, sometimes especially positive change, means you must rock the boat, you stop doing what you are doing now. It's time to stop complaining and *do* something.

Power Mindset

When you learn how to control your mind – in the simplest of ways – your world will turn around and put you in charge. The *110 phil0sophy* will give you your power back! It's all about controlling your mind – ***controlling your thinking***! We aren't taught that. From a young age, we aren't taught how to think, we're taught to follow the rules, do what we're told without question. In school we are taught how to follow directions and how to memorize information, not how to think for ourselves. That's why we are so influenced by the media, other people, apps, games, blogs, all the distractions this world offers us all call our name, seem to care, and tell us what to think. When you stop the flood of external information coming at you, and slow down and *think*, you give yourself an incredible ability to control what happens next! The *110 phil0sophy* teaches how to be thoughtful instead of reactive, how to strategize decisions instead of being captivated by emotions.

This is one of the reasons why this book's pages are going backwards. By flipping pages, it forces you to think differently. I'm trying to reinforce that you have already begun to think differently and are implementing the *110 phil0sophy*.

When we are young, we are taught to color in the lines of the coloring book and what colors we are supposed to color things – that is how you get the gold star on your page, right? But, when we "sacrifice" the gold star in order to color our world however we want, show our unique creativity, that's when we really flourish as an individual. SO, that means working outside the lines and trusting your own creativity is actually how you get the gold star!

The key is to be present, keep a clear mind, and focus on what is happening NOW. Of course, anyone who has tried this knows that is much easier said than done! What you will learn next is a series of techniques and ways to manage your thinking in any situation that will help you sift out the facts from feelings, determine what is in your control that you can change, and set a plan of action for that change, in a series of simple steps. The things that you cannot change, you need to let go of. Stop getting bogged down in them and move on. There is too much happiness to experience to waste your time in "Poor Me Syndrome"!

Did you know an average person makes 35,000 choices per day? Google it! Can you imagine if you just changed 2% of your choices/decisions? That would be 700 different choices. Imagine if all of those changed decisions were now positive decisions. Just imagine how many happier moments you would have in a day, and then in a week, a month, etc!

Thinking versus Feeling

It's important to distinguish what I mean about thinking versus feeling. I'm not talking about not caring or saying that our feelings do not matter. Feelings matter very much! They are fantastic signals to us that something is going on. It might be how much fun we are having, so we are feeling joyous. Or it could be that something is wrong, so our feelings of fear and anxiety are signals for us to be aware of. The issue arises when we give too much credence to our feelings, treating them as our main compass, guiding our actions and responses. One thing you can always count on is that feelings are *temporary*. The passing nature of feelings is why we want to think of them as a street sign, not the roadmap.

Our feelings naturally impact our thinking, but when we give our feelings too much power they impact our thinking in a counter-productive way. We tend to get stuck in the emotions, bypassing rational facts and strategic thinking. When our decisions are made strictly from our emotions, we usually miss very valuable information and fail to consider long-term impacts of our choices. **Think of your emotions as simply triggers, alerting you that something is happening, and it could be good or bad.** Once the feeling triggers you to pay attention, then you turn to your mind to work at dissecting what is happening, is it good for you or bad, and then determine an objective response.

Feelings tell us:

- WOW this is fun! I want more of this in my life!
- Uh-oh, I don't like this! I need to make a change!
- Ohhh, I'm sad (or lonely or overwhelmed), what is happening here?
- Ugh, I'm not happy, what do I need to be doing differently?

Take the day I got a speeding ticket for going too fast through a school zone. At first I was really mad, started down the "poor me" path, but then I realized what I was doing. I was letting that speeding ticket ruin my whole day, and I was spending way too much time stewing over it. I knew I was wrong, I had made a dumb mistake of going too fast, and I just needed to own it and move on. What did I do? I went right to the courthouse and paid it that day! Why wait? Why let it sit on my desk as a reminder of a poor decision and a negative experience?! Each of our actions is reinforcing our future behaviors. I want to reinforce the positive and always be moving forward. By paying that ticket I made a very powerful action in my life to take responsibility, do what needs to be done to get beyond a negative experience, and then *let it go!*

The best use of our feelings is to take them for the wonderful cues that they are, then get on to the thinking process in considering your response – get on to the *solution* phase where we dissect what is really happening, what we need or can do differently, and then ACT!

Thinking Exercises

These exercises are simple, yet powerful. I know because it is how I manage myself every day – day in and day out. I use these techniques for small things like when to schedule an appointment or how I respond to a difficult communication. And I use these techniques for big decisions such as hiring a new staff member. Once you start practicing the *110 phil0sophy* and its methods, they will become second nature; your mind (thinking) will go directly to the sequences of the *110 phil0sophy* techniques. You will finally be free from ruminating and getting stuck in the thought loops of worry, storytelling and catastrophizing – you will control your mind, it will no longer control you!

We make choices all the time about how we are going to think and experience things. We DO have influence over our future, so therefore we can *control* our future. It's a thought process!

For example, what if a co-worker was late in presenting a key report you needed for a meeting, and this consistently happened. Let's figure out the issue – the report is needed each Friday. Now let's dissect why the angered feeling is occurring – my co-worker is consistently late with the report. Also, I'm dependent on my co-worker for this information. And finally, let's figure out how this issue can be corrected – we could create a template so figures could be inserted and the preparation time would be diminished; and quite possibly lead to each co-worker having the tools to complete the report when needed. Instead of spending the afternoon fuming over the event that happened, why not redirect that energy into figuring out what went wrong, what you could have done differently, and then making a plan for change next time something similar happens? Then move on. Get back to your fabulous, precious life!

> *"The biggest hurdle you will ever face is your thinking.*
> *If you can master your thoughts, you can do anything."*

> ~ Luanne Cameron

EXERCISE: Make Time to Think!

I know this sounds silly, but it's not! It's important to make intentional time for thinking. We can get very tangled up in our thoughts when they are "free-form" – worrying in the middle of the night, dwelling on how hurt we feel over an experience, believing we don't have "any choice" about something so we just keep resenting a situation. Sound familiar at all? Sure, we all say, "I need to think about that." But then do we actually *really* do it? Perhaps if there is a big decision on the table we mull it around in our mind when we're driving, in the shower, or at 3:00 a.m. when we should be sleeping. We must have a disciplined structure to apply to our thoughts to make them work in our benefit. Taking intentional, quiet time to think is the first step to controlling our thinking. What I am talking about is making a habit of creating time to think (because we know good habits are very important to success of all this happiness stuff!)

Ways to formalize your Time to Think might include:

- 15 minutes first thing in the morning while you have your cup of coffee

- In the shower or bath

- Taking a lunchtime walk around the block

- While driving or commuting

- While doing laundry, cleaning, chores

- While exercising/working out

- After dinner or during evening "down time"

I highly recommend keeping a journal, notebook or your phone handy to record your thoughts, questions, ideas, etc. during these thinking times! It is important to capture your "big thoughts" and it's very easy to forget about them once you jump back into your busy life. My shower and commuting times are my key daily thinking times. Be creative and use technology. I use talking text to email myself my thoughts and ideas from the shower, when I am working out, or when I am driving so I can capture my big thoughts!

EXERCISE: Basic 110

This exercise will remind you of the *Daily Diagnosis* exercise which was on page 46. This boiled down version is intended to give you a quick response when your thinking is going to excessive worry, over-emotional, or you just need a way to focus. Again, don't forget that the good stuff deserves to be analyzed too – that is how you make sure you incorporate more of it in your life!

When you need to reel yourself back in, ask yourself (write down if possible) answers to these questions:

What's actually happening (just the facts)?

_____

_____

Why is it happening?

_____

_____

What needs to change?

_____

_____

Let's take a look at a few examples of how I use this:

 # 1) Using the example of when I was traveling so much for work. I used to start feeling sick on Sunday afternoon. I was miserable; I was sad; I was homesick before I even left for my trips.

What's actually happening (just the facts)?
I am miserable; I feel sick; I miss my husband and children.

Why is it happening?
Too much travel, too many days at a time.

What needs to change?
I need to talk with my boss and be honest about what was going on with me.

And you know what happened? When I went and talked to my boss, told him honestly what was going on and how miserable I was, he offered to figure out a way to fix things! I renegotiated my position, and we changed my job description some so that I no longer traveled as much. I had been a valuable, hard working employee and they didn't want to lose me. I held to my Guiding Principles, and stood up for myself. Remember, when you don't ask, the answer is always no!

 # 2) Recently I had a tough decision to make in my company. There was a product line that I sold which had been very lucrative for me and my business, and it also offered my customers a very good value with something they needed in their lives. I have a passion to help people, and of course I am in business to make money, so when the regulations and other licensing issues arose that heavily impacted this product line for me, I was faced with the hard decision of whether or not to continue to sell this line of products. It was weighing very heavily on my mind over the course of several months.

What's actually happening (just the facts)?

I would need to spend a lot of time and some investment to continue to sell this line. I would need to get further licensing and would be required to become a broker. Most importantly, my personal responsibilities to my customers if something bad happened in the market would impact my service to my customers. I worry about my customer's money as if it were my own. These products might cause me and distress to my customers.

Why is it happening?

Changing of regulations, completely outside of my control; however, I can control whether or not I take on this added responsibility.

What needs to change?

I want things to be 110% guaranteed and secure for my customers. I do not want to be *worrying* about their financial future. Based on my priorities, I chose to no longer sell this product line. Although it had been profitable and would likely continue to be, my bigger purpose and longevity view for my future career, no longer was in alignment with the new mandated regulations within this product line. The responsibility on me as an individual was not worth jeopardizing my longevity view of happiness.

Remember: When we have *worry*, the question is what we can control. Spend your energy considering only the factors that you can control.

 # 3) How about a positive one to work through – we always want the positive stuff in life to continue so that needs attention as well! I've begun training for this year's Tri for a Cure, now that I am healthy and can do it again.

What's actually happening (just the facts)?

Training is tough, and I have to stay very disciplined in order to make it through the Tri successfully. I am training several days per week to get back in shape – running and biking after work, doing swims on the weekends. I have begun to notice that I feel like a Rock Star!

Why is it happening?

After a few weeks of training I really notice how good I feel. Exercising consistently, several days a week, really makes a difference in how I feel. I'm feeling strong, slender, and energetic. When I am in shape, and disciplined about working out to stay in shape, eating well to be able to work out well, getting enough sleep to recuperate from my workout, I feel great – inside and out.

What needs to change?

I need to be sure to make this an ongoing part of my lifestyle, not just when I am training for the Tri for a Cure. I work to stay in shape, but like everyone, I fall off the wagon. For me, being in shape is a huge part of my Self Guiding Principle priority, and I want this Rock Star feeling to continue!

110 phil0sophy: **DISCIPLINE**

Decision Making

The *110 phil0sophy* is a lot about making good decisions, in-formed decisions that will keep us focused on what is most important to us. While all of us have to make decisions every day, many of us do not have good skills. Good decision-making skills are essential to healthy relationships, parenting, successful careers, and a fulfilling and happy life! I seriously believe that you increase your value as a human being when you are a good decision maker! We need to have the ability to make decisions quickly and responsibly. Decision making is related to planning, organizing, and achieving any goal. You won't get anywhere near your Vision if you don't have good decision-making skills! The real point of having the **Guiding Principles** is for decision making because every decision you make for your day should be weighed against those values, and that order of priority.

Here is a simple example. When I am at work, especially if I am talking with a member of my team or a customer, I don't let personal phone calls interrupt me. However, there is a big differ-ence between a call from my hairstylist and a call from my son. Recently I was in a business meeting and my son called. I didn't pick up. But when he called again 10 minutes later, I excused myself and picked up his call. He knows my policy, and I know he wouldn't call me again unless he really needed to talk to me. Because my family is #4 of my **Guiding Principles** and work is #5, he got priority and my decision was easy to make! That is why the principles outlined in the *110 phil0sophy* work so well – you have a clear set of guidelines and all you need to do is apply them. It makes decision making much faster and less stressful!

It's crucially important that we make *informed* decisions. What do I mean by that? Good decisions require us to get out of our feelings, at least initially, and look at what our options are in an objective way. We often don't even realize what all of our options are! Sometimes, when we don't like an option (or let our feelings interfere) we leave it off the table altogether, but that is a bad habit. You may not like all of your options, but you still need to consider them in the bigger picture of making an informed decision. Once you have applied logic to your decision, outlined all the facts, then you can add in your personal feelings about the situation. It shouldn't take center stage, however, until you have analyzed the decision rationally.

I think it's important to classify decisions into whether they are business decisions or personal decisions. Business decisions tend to be more objective and based on facts and data, whereas personal decisions likely include a lot more emotion, a balance between emotional and objective (using facts and data).

So when I'm faced with a decision, the first thing I do is classify it as "business" or "personal." This helps me decide what priorities the decision is impacting. Once I know what bucket the decision is in, I can move through the decision-making process faster. Of course, many business decisions, such as my decision about whether to continue to sell that product line that I described back a few pages, involve both facts and feelings. In that example, it couldn't be all business facts because my customers' lives were involved and that factor to me was very personal (part of my values).

Characteristics of a Good Decision Maker:

➤ Has a clear set of priorities. You must know what your values are in order to choose the "right" decision for you. That's where the Guiding Principles come in!

➤ Looks at a situation rationally, separating out the facts from feelings.

➤ Is flexible and open minded to other ways of thinking, other options and other ways of doing things.

> ➤ Listens well to other opinions when a decision will affect other people.

> ➤ Can be realistic about potential outcomes of a decision. Not all choices are preferred, but sometimes are necessary (needing surgery for example).

What about intuition – that "gut feeling" that you should or shouldn't do something? Listen to it! While I stand firm that good decisions are rational decisions, I completely believe in intuition. There are a lot of scientific facts for not over thinking and listening to your gut or first inclination. Responding to test questions is a good example. I do believe we all have intuition, gut senses that guide us. When I was living with my mother and my abusive stepfather, my intuition was screaming at me to get away from there. I was too young to really understand intellectually what was going on, and I certainly had no means to take care of myself, yet I *knew* I had to get away. I couldn't have described exactly what was wrong, but I knew something was wrong and I needed to get out. So I ran away from home.

It is often a good idea, and for many of us extraverts, a downright need, to seek the input of others whose opinion we value. This can be a slippery slope for a couple reasons. First, someone else, no matter how close they are to you, does not have your same priorities or needs. They also might not have the right experience and knowledge to make a good decision about certain situations. They may also have a vested interest in the outcome, and therefore influence you based on what they want or need, not what you want or need. You might have a few close confidantes that you seek advice from, but remember to keep your decisions to what is right for you, not someone else.

EXERCISE: 3-Strike Rule

One of my favorite *110 phil0sophy* "rules" is the 3-Strike Rule. I use it a lot in my business, as well as life. It means that I watch for patterns in my experiences, and when I see something undesirable occur that is not requiring an immediate remedy, I simply pay attention to whether it continues to happen. If that experience, or some variation of it, occurs a third time, it's out and I need to do something else.

Because, of course, life happens, right?! So I don't over-react to issues, I ask myself, "Is this the first time it's happened? The second? The third?" The first time an unpleasant or undesirable situation occurs, I might need to just let it go. It might just be mine or someone's learning curve in action, something I should just let go, shake it off. BUT, if this is the second time then I really start to hone in on the situation. What is happening? Why is this happening again? I recognize something might be up so I automatically pay closer attention and resolve it if possible. I also begin to think of contingency plans. Then if it occurs a third time, I consider it a challenge that needs to be dealt with *now*, and I already have determined my other options so I can quickly resolve it. Because I have already worked on the solutions before the third occurrence, I don't waste time in the emotion or frustration of the event which would impact my ability to figure out my course of action.

- **1ˢᵗ Time Occurrence**: Is this a big deal? Just someone learning or making a mistake?

- **2ⁿᵈ Time Occurrence**: Uh-oh, something might be up. What is happening? Why? What should have happened instead/done differently? What are my other options? What will my plan of action be if this happens a 3ʳᵈ time?

- **3ʳᵈ Occurrence**: Take immediate action to correct the issue.

This process is a great best-practice in your organization, or anywhere individuals are learning! It teaches people to speak up when things don't happen or feel right, puts disciplined thinking into place to analyze what is happening, and empowers people to figure out what needs to change for them.

In my career, I've coached a lot of new managers who are just figuring out how to act, how to make decisions, how to handle conflict. For example, a manager might have an employee who makes a poor decision. Let's say they write a letter with the wrong dates in it. Not necessarily a huge deal, but it looks sloppy and un-professional. The manager catches it and corrects it with the employee. Then it happens a second time. This time, the manager needs to document it, talk more fully to the employee about the mistake, and develop a plan of action should the mistake happen a third time. They decide their reaction before the problem escalates, before they are in the heat of the moment. At work, this process keeps everyone very professional, very fair, and very even tempered. This is also a great practice because when you decide what your response is going to be *before* a third strike occurs, you are making decisions when you are calmer and more level-headed. The *3-Strike Rule* helps you to not over-react and you are ready to execute resolution immediately on the 3rd time when you need it.

"Gain strength in your past. It will help you through challenges in the present, and serve to vastly improve your future!"
~ Luanne Cameron

110 phil0sophy: DISCIPLINE

Problem Solving

Problem solving is different than decision-making. Problem solving occurs when we are forced to make a decision because of circumstances that are creating an undesirable situation. Decision making is choosing something because you *want* it, problem solving occurs because there is a situation occurring that you *do not* want. Problem solving begins as babies; it's how we learn to walk. As adults, problems get more complex, and good skills which analyze and solve those problems help tremendously in daily life whether we're trying to keep mice out of the attic or figuring out how to work with a difficult co-worker.

Problems are what cause fights in marriages and make teenagers unbearable. Problems are what plague most managers at work all day, every day. Problems are at the center of most of our unhappiness! Since problems seem to monopolize much of our daily life, having fast and easy problem-solving skills would basically be a game-changer, right?!

First off, I don't like the word "problem." I prefer to use the terms "challenge" or "issue." I think a "problem" is always an opportunity to learn! I am not being trite, here. Our greatest source of learning occasions come from things we see as problems – situation we don't like or enjoy. When you think or hear the word "problem" associated with a situation, let that be an immediate trigger to yourself to change the terminology to "challenge." The word "problem" is just steeped in negativity, but the word "challenge," by formal definition, means "to defy or dispute." Perfect! The power in changing your language, and therefore your attitude, from problem to challenge, changes your whole perspective. Your mind shifts to viewing it as something you can overcome.

Utilizing the methods of the *110 phil0sophy*, you will learn to quickly assess a challenge, determine other options, and take the necessary actions to make a change occur. One way or another, I promise you, all ~~problems~~ challenges have solutions!

Good Problem Solving involves:

- ➢ Understanding what is happening
- ➢ Identifying what we want to change or improve
- ➢ Diagnosing why things occurred as they did
- ➢ Analyzing alternative approaches
- ➢ Deciding on the best alternative approach
- ➢ Taking the necessary actions to implement changes
- ➢ Observing the impact of the new actions – was the problem solved?

Never skip reflecting on the teaching that a ~~problem~~ challenge provided. This is a big mistake people make. We are so relieved to be rid of the ~~problem~~ issue that we can't wait to just move on and forget about it. Always take the time to process the impact the ~~problem~~ challenge had, what you learned from it, how the solution worked, and what can still be improved upon after an incident. Keep adjusting accordingly.

EXERCISE: S.A.P.S.
(Situational Analysis for Problem Solving)

I absolutely love a problem-solving technique I developed that I call **S.A.P.S. (Situational Analysis for Problem Solving)**. It allows you to calm down and focus on the facts. You will be less distracted by emotions and drama around the situation. It creates the mechanism to consider your existing resource which is fantastic because sometimes you discover something you didn't realize you had available to you. It's a great training opportunity for your team (and for you!). And it's *FAST* so you can get back to life and work!

The S.A.P.S. exercise provides an invaluable tool that allows you to break down the circumstances of a situation so it can be managed successfully. It can be done quickly so you stop wasting time complaining or regretting, and get on to solving the issue. Do not skip paying attention to the learning opportunity from the experience so you can avoid, or at least be prepared to manage it, in the future!

The S.A.P.S. exercise puts you immediately into problem solving mode, because we immediately distinguish the circumstances surrounding the situation between the things we can control versus the things we can't control. This is important. Time after time, we get stuck worrying, complaining and thinking about parts of issues that we *can not* control. What a waste of time and energy! Using the S.A.P.S. diagram, you can immediately identify all the components of the situation, and separate them into these two categories. We know right away that the things we can't control we need to just accept and move on from. They are not worth our energy. Now, the focus becomes on the right side of the diagram – what we *can* control about what is going on.

In this example, I had a situation where the pipes in the vacant offices next to mine had frozen and my whole office area flooded. We couldn't use our offices, but I needed to service my customers and keep my business operating. We could have become really bogged down in lamenting the whole "Why us?!" scenario, but that was pointless. Instead, we mapped out what we could control in the situation – and utilized our previously built in disaster recovery business plan we had developed when we were not in a crisis situation. I immediately called my business peers, rerouted our phone calls, borrowed some offices from another large firm and we had flexibility already built in to be able to have my team work from home.

Let's review the process for good challenge solving. Here is my example of the freezing pipes incident:

CIRCUMSTANCES	
CAN'T Control	**CAN Control**
• Quickly list out what parts of the situation are outside of your control.	• Quickly list out what parts of the situation you do have control over.
Ex: Employee Quits Ex: Water Pipes Burst	Ex: Speak with Team, talk to peers; reach out to resources. Know standard operating policies.
Let these things GO!	**Determine your steps to change and address them.**

EXERCISE

S.A.P.S. (Situational Analysis for Problem Solving)

Try analyzing your own situation:

CIRCUMSTANCES	
CAN'T Control	**CAN Control**
• Quickly list out what parts of the situation are outside of your control.	• Quickly list out what parts of the situation you do have control over.
Let these things GO!	➢ **Circle the best option(s).** ➢ **Determine your steps to make the necessary changes.**

110 phil0sophy: DISCIPLINE

Worrying – Your Cue to Contingency Plan

What if I told you worrying is a *good thing*? Well, it is! What isn't good is hanging on to our worry, spinning around and around in self-doubt, dramatizing and catastrophizing, over thinking things to the point of paralysis (and to no end). That's where we get stuck. If you think of worry as a yellow caution flag, however, waving "Hello! Pay attention!" at you, then worry simply becomes a tap on your shoulder that you need to do something. Where worry is concerned, what you need to do is make contingency plans.

Caution! Worrying in Progress!

Worry stems from the feeling of fear, manifesting as anxiety, stress and frustration. When we are frightened about something, we feel out of control, life is unpredictable, and at our deepest core that feels *bad*. Humans like control, control means we are safe and secure, we are ok. If you buy into your feelings only, you get stuck there and forget you have the power to think as well. You can get trapped and start believing that your worries will come true. Remember – feelings are temporary (and often lying to us)! If you, instead, see your worry as simply a cue then you take your power back, employ your ability to think, and can move through the emotions and onto the solutions phase. The *110 phil0sophy* LOVES solutions!

I personally like when I realize I am worrying. I've come to greatly appreciate it as an early warning sign – like intuition is to my "gut feelings." Let's look at two techniques I use to turn my worry into action – **Contingency Planning** and **Planned Distraction**.

Contingency Planning and Planned Distraction are different from the S.A.P.S. exercise because S.A.P.S. is about dealing with a situation at hand – something (unforeseen) has happened that creates challenges to deal with, whereas Contingency Planning and Planned Distraction are exercises for you to do when there is an impending circumstance coming, something you are not looking forward to or are worrying about heading your way (or perceived to be heading your way).

Things legitimately go wrong in life. The amazing ability humans have is that before things even go wrong, we start to worry about them going wrong! We make up all sorts of stories about what is going to happen, what people are going to say to us, how awful life is going to become. Contingency Planning is all about removing unnecessary worries and ineffective stressors. It's about stopping the cycle of useless fretting, and instead letting worry simply trigger you to turn that energy into planning other alternatives should things go wrong. When you set Plan A, B and C, determine other solutions to get your desired outcome, you take back your power over any situation. You don't have to torture yourself anymore – use these *110 phil0sophy* techniques to harness the energy of worry into productive actions that will make you feel better *instantly* – I promise!

EXERCISE: Contingency Planning

Describe the situation you are worrying about:

_____

What, specifically, am I worrying about? Describe your worries, individually, in detail:

1. _____

2. _____

3. _____

4. _____

For each individual worry, what are the potential responses (contingency plans) I can choose? Remember to focus on what you can control.

Worry # 1

_____

_____

_____

_____

Worry # 3

_____

_____

_____

_____

Worry # 2

_____

_____

_____

Worry # 4

_____

_____

_____

Go into each worry box and circle your most preferred solution. Like all good contingency plans, you may need a Plan A, Plan B, and so on...

Let me walk you through one of my recent worries:

I recently needed to have major surgery on both my feet. For one foot, it would be the second surgery because my undiagnosed autoimmune illness caused my first surgery to not be successful, so I had to repeat it. Well, I knew what was coming and I was dreading it! I was worried that I was going to be totally out of work, flat on my back with my leg raised above my heart, for 8 weeks. I had a business to keep running in my absence. I was going to be in pain and would have to take pain killers. I would be dependent on people for much of my needs, and I was not going to be able to perform or work at all for weeks. Looking at each of my major worries independently, I made some plans based on what I could control about each area:

- For pain, I accepted that I needed to take pain medication. I learned from my previous surgery experiences that I would need to keep to a regular schedule in order to control the pain. I bought one of those timer covers so I could see very clearly when I had taken a pain pill, and knew when it was time to take another.

- To address my lack of dependence, I designed my surroundings to better serve the need to take care of myself to some degree. I bought a good shower chair so I had stability in the shower to be there alone. The chair gave me greater comfort so I could enjoy my bathing, relax and breathe in the steam, and overall feel more independence about this activity. I also put a mini refrigerator right in my room to keep snacks and drinks handy so I wouldn't have to be dependent on people for little things like a cold drink.

- I knew this would be stressful on my family (caregivers) as well, so I implemented my office best practices into the home. I bought little gift bags to present to my caregivers for when they were tired. I would invite them to select a 'grab bag' from a basket. It was a fun, practical thank you gift.

- I made sure I had really good, experienced coverage for my business. I knew I wouldn't be able to contribute, so I needed someone whom I trusted and who knew what they were doing so I wouldn't have to be answering questions or worrying about what was going on at my office.

EXERCISE: Planned Distraction

Often times worry stems from anticipation of something un-pleasant – an upcoming medical test or surgery, difficult conversations or confrontations, going on a blind date. When you are worrying about something that you cannot do anything about, or you have done your preparation and now it's just a waiting game, the best use of your time is to *not* worry about it. The easy way to do that is by distracting yourself. The power of the *110 phil0sophy* is that we interrupt these feelings and worrying by intentionally planning a solution – we *plan distractions*.

When I am heading into something I am dreading or worrying about, I plan distractions for myself, things that really take my mind off the issue at hand, and keep my mind and my body occupied until the looming event. Take my cancer surgery, for example. Obviously something that I was not looking forward to, was fraught with tons of worries; and they were primarily things I could not control until the surgery was over and the test results were back. SO, after I had completed my Contingency Planning (set my affairs and paperwork in order, scheduled my recuperation time and coverage at work, packed my hospital bag), there was nothing to do but wait.

Here's a look at my Planned Distractions:

- I knew I would be depending on other people to take care of the laundry and put away my clothes, so I took that as an opportunity to really clean out my closets and drawers. I organized my closet by type of clothing – pants together, shirts in a row. Then, with neatly folded drawers of clothing and accessories, I labeled the outside of my drawers as to what went where so whoever was putting things away would know where to put them.

- I cleaned, cleaned, cleaned! The physical work of cleaning kept me busy and wore me out to some degree. I like the results I can see when I clean, and that made me feel that I was accomplishing something, and having the house so clean carried us through several weeks after surgery.

- I scheduled time with friends that included a walk, a massage or a great meal. Since I'd be flat on my back for a while, sitting at a pretty table eating dinner, getting a great massage or walking through a wooded trail connected me with activities I love, and it gave me a chance to visit with my friends before I was out of commission for many weeks.

- I shopped for new lounge clothes, reading materials, and other things to use during my recuperation. Things that would be fun to put on or read for the first time, things that made me happy, or more relaxed, marking my successful journey through my recovery.

- When I would get really down or worried, I would put on my headphones and listen to uplifting music, and inspirational podcasts. I would pray or meditate to connect to my greater purpose, reminding myself, this too shall pass.

"The nice thing about rain,

is that it stops… Eventually."

~ Eeyore

110 phil0sophy: **FINAL THOUGHTS**

The Importance of Practice

No improvement comes without practice. The Beatles weren't "fabulous" the first time they played together, athletes don't make the Olympics and win medals until they put lots of time and energy into perfecting their skills. To be even decent at something, you need practice. To become really good, to make any lasting change, you need to practice, practice, practice! Practice is all about repetition, which is the same as routine. Just like any other muscle, your mind needs the same routine, to repeat the same exercises, processes, mantras, over and over to train (perhaps retrain) and strengthen it!

You must practice these *110 phil0sophy* approaches to life for it to have lasting impact. They are really quality checks and balances for your life, built into every *110 phil0sophy* approach and exercise. You must do the exercises in this book over and over again, applying discipline to your decision-making and problem-solving.... Soon when that feeling of "Oh something is wrong here" or "I don't like this" occurs, it will raise that yellow flag in your mind telling you to stop and pay attention to what is going on. Now you will have a disciplined way to address these things – move from emotional feelings of anxiety or fear to *controlling your thinking about things* so you can figure out what to do differently in the future. You will be able to move through situations much more quickly the more you practice. You will recognize an issue, think it through, and then get through it. You can't go from floating around aimlessly, unhappy in life, with no Vision, to a powerful, in-charge individual without practice!

Plan for the future, but live for today....

"Working with Luanne has been an eye-opening experience. As a young agent looking back at my first few years I can honestly say I was successful by mistake at times, but after working with Luanne I can now say I do things systematically and with the end in mind. Whether it's monitoring monthly agency premium/book growth, or building an office culture, Luanne has assisted me in creating a sustainable business that will continue to grow, the right way, for many years to come."

~ Bobby Donnelly, Previous Small Business Owner;
Presently, Sales Field Executive

110 phil0sophy: CONCLUSION

The *110 phil0sophy* is a *"Be Happy" Philosophy*

- Create a clear vision that you are excited about!

- Be 110% engaged.

- Don't compromise your Guiding Principles and priorities.

- Control your thinking – manage negative thoughts and experiences and turn them around into action steps.

- Maintain good problem-solving techniques to get back on track quickly and avoid distractions.

- Always have a contingency plan.

- Keep visuals around you that remind you of your vision and goals.

- Track results, learn from mistakes and successes, adapt and adjust as necessary.

- Practice the *110 phil0sophy* over and over so it becomes second nature

- Constantly cultivate more and more happiness in your life!

- **Be YOU!**

Keep in mind the importance of our own self-improvement…**you deserve to be a top priority**. If you don't make yourself a top priority, who will?

We teach people how to treat us; we are a role model all the time. My focus in all aspects of my life – personal and business – is on people, processes, and paying attention to results. My deep values center on being a role model, giving back, and helping people. How I spend my time better supports those desires. I do this by having a structure to my priorities and discipline to be consistently putting effort into accomplishing what is important.

How do you know if you are doing a good job? Well, you have to analyze and measure your results – are you doing better, worse, or what needs to be adjusted? The key is to maintain consistency in your efforts.

Always remember the importance of Vision. Something that is front and center, all the time – that does not change.

And remember, if I didn't have the Vision I had for my life – to live to be 110 years young – I would not have stepped out of my corporate executive life when I had the opportunity in the "Great Recession" to find a better balance. I would have never had the mammogram that uncovered the breast cancer. If I hadn't stayed positive with my Vision through the breast cancer, I would not have chosen the aggressive treatment with reconstructive breast surgery that uncovered how ill I really was, uncovering the two benign neck tumors. And, if I didn't have the Vision of not being in a wheelchair due to pain in my feet – I would have NEVER had the additional foot surgeries, on top of everything else I had just lived through.

ALL of that crazy, on top of a childhood of craziness, allowed me the opportunity of numerous life experiences and the time for me to articulate through writing with a passion; to believe in paying the positive forward and helping 110 individuals' journey be just a little easier!

Perhaps that is my purpose in life – to share my challenges and way of navigating my own compass to help push others forward on their personal journey. If this book helped you by just 1%, I've helped with 350 choices. (That's 1% of the 35,000 choices you make on an average every day). And .003143% of those number of choices would equal 110 choices – just imagine!

Are you 1 of the 110 individuals who can implement in your life or business just .003143% of this *110 phil0sophy*?

Dedications

The Guiding Principles are such an important part of my *110 phil0sophy*, it seems appropriate to reinforce the principles by using them to dedicate my heartfelt appreciation for making my dream come true!

Spiritual – God

I dedicate this book to God and His team of angels who helped me to remain strong and incredibly optimistic during all of my life's challenges. He helped me find my true purpose in life.

Self – ME

By delivering this book to help others be their best, ironically, as I finish and cross the 1 – 10 – 2020, the delivery date deadline, I never really realized how much I needed to write this book, to place so many of my personal challenges on the "Shelf". Now instead of having to share all the details of what makes me special – the challenges that have developed my perseverance – I can simply say, "Read my book, the *110 phil0sophy*!"

For those who have lived through childhood crisis, health crisis and/or a life crisis, you will understand the value of not having to tell your personal story over and over again. How refreshing for me to finally totally move on!

Spouse – JP

Words cannot describe how blessed I am to have you by my side always. You are always in front of me when I need direction and behind me when I need that stubborn kick in the butt. But most importantly, thank you, JP, for being my best friend throughout all of the ups and downs of our life journey together.

Thank you for totally "Getting Me!" and loving me for me – the great, the not so great, and the absolute ugly in me.

Family/Friendships

Thank you, Dad, for being such an inspiration to take care of myself and to ensure I live a fulfilled life in the best physical and spiritual shape ever. Thank you, Sally, for being my dad's best friend and silent anchor in life.

Thank you, Mom, for teaching me the gift of true happiness through your tragedies. I have unleashed the secret recipe to happiness, not only for me now, but for the entire world.

Thank you to my children for all of your encouragement throughout the years, especially by putting my story out there for all to learn from. And thank you for loving me – for the quirky mom that I am – not always the best in all areas, especially in the kitchen. But thank you for loving the FFY as much as I do! Thank you for giving me a hug just when I needed it or a call home to just "check in" on me!

Thank you to all my brothers for your ongoing support through all the ups, but mostly when I was down.

Thank you to all of my friends throughout my life journey. I so appreciate your shoulders to lean on, your ears to listen and your words of wisdom.

Career

Thank you, Lyndon State College, who offered me a stepping stone to become a BS graduate from the School of Nursing, Therapeutic Recreation Therapy at the University of Southern Maine. Thank you, USM, for building my intellectual confidence that my degree allowed me to pursue the career success that I have experienced and more than ever dreamed possible.

www. 110PhilOsophy.com

About the Author

Luanne Cameron is a Business & Life Strategist. She is an entrepreneur, small business coach, author and public speaker. Her goal is to teach people about the principles that have brought her success, and to help others realize their own through her tried and true practices and techniques.

Luanne is best known for her veracious belief in her business philosophy of creating work environments that inspire and energize individuals in a team environment.

She opened her own insurance agency in 2011, after a successful corporate career. With her business success, and having survived breast cancer, Luanne is more determined than ever to share her belief that we can live life to the fullest and achieve success through a balanced life-work approach to setting priorities, making decisions, and navigating through difficult circumstances.

Highlights of her career include:

- 30+ years leadership roles in the insurance industry.
- Implemented three front-line operational service centers for three Fortune 500 companies, managing over 150 employees with >3%turnover and a $6.5M budget within 2% variance.
- Developed cross-functional teams to implement and promote a culture of customer service excellence.
- Owns and operates Cameron Insurance Agency, Inc., a successful State Farm agency in Standish, Maine.
- Awards & Recognition:

  ~ Legion of Honor–Bronze Tablet Ambassador Travel Top 100/ Retirement Products President's Club/Top 50 Agents 2016

  ~ Nominated for Chairman's Award from a large insurance company.

As stated throughout the book, Luanne's personal Vision is to live to be 110 years young, all the while being engaged 110% in everything she does in service to her vision, and have fun all the while!

Luanne's professional Vision is to share her experiences and best practices with others so that they can achieve more happiness and satisfaction in their careers and personal lives!

The 110 phil0sophy and the Work Culture

The *110 phil0sophy* is a useful tool for any type of business management. Work culture is so critical to business success. The Guiding Principles of this philosophy will help company leaders unite personal and business priorities so that employees have ownership of the company's vision and long-term goals.

Numerous articles and studies have shown that American workers are overworked, stressed, and suffering from a lack of meaning at work. According to the <u>Harvard Business Review</u>, "Most executives have an opportunity to liberate at least 20% of their employees' time by bringing greater discipline to time management." The *110 phil0sophy* is the tool managers need to unleash workers' productivity.

A. **VISION** – For the company and the employee's personal life, vision is essential. Throughout my life, I've learned and taught the importance of vision at work and at home. Personally, my rocky childhood taught me to pursue a family life that was stable and emotionally healthy for my children. In the office, I have led numerous teams and organizations to financial success by honing a concise, compelling organizational vision that inspires team members to give 110% of their abilities and focus to the task at hand.

B. **ENGAGEMENT** – Have fun! Life is short and much of it is spent at work. Creating a positive work environment with perks, games, and opportunities to socialize keeps employees engaged and committed to the company. My education in therapeutic recreation taught me that fun activities offer the best opportunities to learn, retain information, and stay focused.

C. **STUCTURE AND DISCIPLINE** – The clock provides structure to our lives every day. Discipline flows from a commitment to our vision and will help us stay committed to our daily structure. The *110 phil0sophy* acknowledges that time is limited, so we must stay disciplined at work and at home to achieve our personal and business goals. When my kids were young, I strived to ensure they were never the last ones left at day care. This required dedicated focus at the office, moving steadily through the work in front of me, and keeping meetings to their scheduled times.

D. THE OFFICE CREED – The process of creating an office creed allows your team to consider what truly matters to them at work and what motivates them to succeed. Creating an office creed with your employees allows them to buy-in to your office's mission, build their engagement in the company's long-term goals, and help them develop a reason to stay focused on following a structure that leads to long-term success. You can develop an office creed in any work environment. I've used this process successfully as a mid-level administrator, a senior executive, and as a business owner. You can always take time to better engage your employees and be a better leader.

For more information, refer to my website:
www.110Philosophy.com

Powerful Hidden Visuals

Within the Book's Cover

If you look very closely to the capital letter "P" on the back cover, you will see the "Breast Cancer" ribbon symbol. This little pink ribbon saved my life! The pink ribbon gave me an acute awareness that getting my routine mammogram was critical in early breast cancer detection – which increases your survivor statistics – which increases your longevity!

AND, if I didn't get breast cancer and, thanks to God, remain positive, I would have never discovered the rare immune disease, Super Hyperparathyroidism, which was hidden for at least 23 years (possibly my entire life). So every time I see this little pink ribbon, I feel so incredibly blessed!

Thank you for sharing my *110 phil0sophy* with your family, friends, and business colleagues so we may all make the world a little more positive. Let them know it is that book with the little green "Turtle" on the cover!

For each book sold, I am donating 110 pennies to cancer research and to foundations that support cancer survivorship as my way of giving back and paying it forward to make the world a better place!

NOTES

NOTES

Colossians 1:10
So that you may live a life worthy of the Lord
and please him in every way;
bearing fruit in every good work,
growing in the knowledge of God.

This page is dedicated to GOD
and His team of angels who helped me
remain strong and incredibly optimistic
during all of my life challenges.

May God continue to keep a special eye
on this little "Turtle"!